CHASE THOMPSON

The Bible and Racism

What the Bible REALLY Says About Racism

Contents

1

Introduction

When I was 8 years old, I asked my parents if I could invite a friend over from school. I told them His name was Alex, and he was a very nice guy, so they said yes. I have no memory of what kind of response they had when Alex actually came home with me, but I honestly don't remember any reaction from either one of them, nor did I ever consider that there might be a reaction. Alex was black, you see, but that fact was really quite insignificant to me, even though we both lived in Birmingham, Alabama, and this was a mere 25 years or so after 'Bull' Connor had loosed the hounds on African-American protesters in our city.

My first real exposure to the evils of racism would happen a few weeks later, when my dad casually told me that some neighbors had seen Alex and I playing in front of my parent's posh Vestavia Hills home, and called to complain. Even as an 8 year old, I was dumbfounded, and couldn't really believe that somebody would be offended just because I had a friend that looked somewhat different than I did. I was a pretty naive kid, I guess.

I suspect that this particular incident was not Alex's first exposure to racism, however. I imagine that racial discrimination and racial animus were regular and everyday facts of life for Alex's family. I, on the other hand, had the privilege of growing up in a situation where, as far as I knew, nobody treated me poorly because of the color of my skin. Alex didn't have that privilege.

To a large degree, I maintained an unhealthy level of naivety to racial issues as I grew up and became an adult. I had plenty of black friends, but I never deeply discussed issues of race with them, essentially thinking that the best way to handle racism was to act completely neutral to skin color, and to personally work on not being a racist myself. I thought that might be enough, but I thought wrong.

Just a few years ago, I realized that maintaining a quietly neutral attitude about race and racism wasn't going to cut it. A small part of that realization was a discussion I had with a good friend, who happens to be black and very conservative politically. My friend is the opposite of an alarmist, and seems to be easily aggravated by those who can find racism in every institution and every action. Thus, I was quite surprised the day he told me that he was frequently pulled over by the police and questioned for no good reason. My friend has a Master's degree, and is a teacher. He drives a car at least as good as mine, probably better. (I drive a 2011 Chevy HHR, if you are curious.) He lives in a good neighborhood and is not a criminal. There's really no reason in the world for him to have far more police interaction than myself, but he assures me that the same is true for all of his black friends. The same is NOT true for all of my white friends. I realized after that conversation that I was now still almost as racially naive as I was when I was a kid. I resolved then to change that dynamic and dive deeper into the scriptural teachings on race and racism, and to consider the ongoing implications of those teachings. The book you are holding is largely the result of the last few years of reading Scripture and seeking out the wisdom of God on race and racism.

My name is Chase, and I am a husband, father, writer, pastor and college professor. This is my fourth published book, and I am very grateful that you took the time to buy it, borrow it, steal it, or whatever. I was born in the 1970's, right in the middle of one of the great epicenters of racism in the world, Birmingham, Alabama. Being American, being a male, being white, being southern, and being in my 40s, limits my perspective on a lot of issues, and I am trying to write with an awareness of all of my cultural limitations and blinders. I will probably fail in several places, but I ask for your grace in those areas, as you are limited and sight challenged also – just in different areas.

If you find errors or egregious opinions in here, OR, if you find content that you want to interact with me about, then PLEASE DO! Going forward, I intend to write my books in a far more interactive way, even including a final chapter in every book that is specifically designed for YOUR input, questions, criticisms, and comments. So, if you are one of the first to buy the book, be sure to check back with Amazon from time to time for version 2, which will contain interactions with readers. The Kindle/ebook version of those updates should be absolutely free. I'd like to be able to do that for the print book as well, but I don't know how to do that yet. (Perhaps I'll make a habit of posting the final chapter of each book on my website.) The way to contact me with your comments, criticisms, and questions is through my site: www.ChaseaThompson.com, or via Facebook. Email works too: chaseathompson@gmail.com. My goal is to publish several pages of interaction with readers, and I will try to let you know if your question will be included.

This is not groundbreaking material nor is it meant to be. The trouble with Christians is not that we need new revelation on issues of race, but that we keep deviating from the clear teachings of the Bible on race, racism, slavery etc. The goal of this book is not to break new ground, nor present new theories, nor to discover long hidden secrets. The goal of this book is to clearly, simply, and passionately proclaim biblical truths about race, and let those truths propel us into action, unity, and peacemaking.

Family Picture, Easter 2017.

If you are interested in my personal life, then here is a paragraph on that. I was blessed to marry Janet, my college sweetheart, in 1995, and together we have five children: Chloe Anna (16), Abbey (14), John Caedmon (13), Kassidy (10), and Phoebe (6). I went to school at Samford University, graduating in 1994 with degrees in History and Philosophy. Following that, I then attended seminary, first at Beeson Divinity, then at Liberty Theological Seminary, graduating in 2006 with a Master of Arts degree in Biblical Studies and another Master's degree a few years later. I have been in ministry since 1992 when I first served as the Junior High Youth Pastor at Hilldale Baptist Church. I have served several churches in the South in a variety of roles: Church planter, Youth Pastor, Teaching Pastor, and even Children's pastor. I am currently pastor of Agape Baptist in Northeast Birmingham, Alabama and have been in that role since February of 2008. I am also an adjunct college professor, and teach New Testament, Old Testament, and history classes.

Thank you for reading! If you are interested in more of my work – including several upcoming volumes in the *What the Bible Really Says* series, please check out my author page on Amazon.com

(www.amazon.com/Chase-Thompson/e/B06Y16M3Q3/) Or visit my web page: www.Chaseathompson.com/blog. Thank you!

Addendum: What is Racism?

In order to discuss racism, it is important to actually define the term upfront, particularly so since there is a movement underway to try and redefine what exactly racism entails. When I use the word racism in this book, I will be using it in the sense that the *Concise Oxford English Dictionary* defines the word. To wit, racism is a noun that means:

1 *The belief that each race or ethnic group possesses specific characteristics, abilities, or qualities that distinguish it as inferior or superior to another such group.*
2 *Discrimination against or antagonism towards other races or ethnic groups based on such a belief (Source: Catherine Soanes and Angus Stevenson, eds., Concise Oxford English Dictionary (Oxford: Oxford University Press, 2004).*

As to current efforts to redefine the word "racism," I wholeheartedly agree with Scott Clark's post on the Heidleblog:

More recently a re-definition has been proposed wherein racism is said to be less about thinking and doing and more about being. It has come to be re-defined in terms of privilege and class, which are Marxist terms of analysis. According to the re-definition then, one is a racist simply by virtue of where and what and when one is, regardless of what one thinks, says, or does. It is a state from which one can never escape. In theological terms, the re-definition is a law from which there is no redemption.

This redefinition is untrue and unhelpful and should be rejected. Nevertheless, this is not to dismiss the sin of racism. Indeed, one reason why the re-definition should be rejected is that it unintentionally and ironically relieves individuals of their moral duty to acknowledge the reality of racism, to repent of it, and to fight against it. (Scott Clark, August 24, 2017. Source: heidelblog.net/)

Scott is correct that there is a great deal of Marxist philosophy that underlies much of the modernist attempts to categorize racism in a different way. I believe, along with the *Oxford English Dictionary*, that it is possible for a person of any race to be a racist – all that is required for that is that one would display discrimination or antagonism against another race simply by virtue of them being a member of that race. Under the OED definition, a white person can be a racist, as can a black person, or a Hispanic person, or an Asian person, etc. I agree with this, and reject modern attempts to re-frame racism as something that only the dominant race in a particular society can be guilty of. That said, when a dominant race *is* guilty of racism, that racism becomes particularly egregious and harmful and abominable, as it takes on a murderous element of bullying. The majority race in any country or culture should vigilantly take great care to quash the evils of racism; unfortunately, the history of most Western cultures demonstrates the opposite of that principle.

2

As Slaves Among the Slaves

At the time when Leonard Dober set out from Herrnhut, not a single other Protestant Church in the world had attacked the task of foreign missions, or even regarded that task as a Divinely appointed duty. In England, Anglicans, Independents and Baptists were all more or less indifferent. In Scotland the subject was never mentioned; and even sixty years later a resolution to inquire into the matter was rejected by the General Assembly {1796.}. In Germany the Lutherans were either indifferent or hostile. In Denmark and Holland the whole subject was treated with contempt. And the only Protestant Church to recognize the duty was this little, struggling Renewed Church of the Brethren.

In this sense, therefore, and in this sense only, can we call the Moravians the pioneers of modern missions. They were the first Protestant Church in Christendom to undertake the conversion of the heathen. They sent out their missionaries as authorized agents of the Church. They prayed for the cause of missions in their Sunday Litany. They had several missionary hymns in their Hymn-Book. They had regular meetings to listen to the reading of missionaries' diaries and letters. They discussed missionary problems at their Synods. They appointed a Church Financial Committee to see to ways and means. They sent out officially appointed "visitors" to inspect the work in various countries. They were, in a word, the first Protestant Missionary Church in history; and thus they set an inspiring example to all their stronger sisters. (Source: A History of the Moravian Church, by Joseph E. Hutton. 1909)

Neither David Nitschmann nor Leonard Dober are household names among Christians in modern times, but they are two of the most influential and brave Christians who have ever lived. Dober was a German pottery maker, who converted to Christianity after visiting the Moravians in Herrnhut ("The Lord's Watch") when he was a teenager. During his mid-twenties, he was stirred greatly by the call of Count Nicholas Von Zinzendorf to world missions and the passion of a former black slave named Anthony Ulrich to see his family members, slaves in the West Indies, won to Christ. Here's the story of how Dober and Nitschmann came to be among the first ever modern foreign missionaries sent out by any church group in Europe:

"In the early part of the last century, a slave on the Danish Island of St. Thomas, frequently sat, after the labours of the day, on the seashore and earnestly sighed for knowledge of the gospel, concerning which he had caught some imperfect notions from the professions of the Europeans, though no man cared for HIS soul, or for the souls of thousands of his fellow-sufferers perishing for lack of knowledge. It was not long after, that his master took him from the island, and brought him to Copenhagen. There he heard the good tidings of great joy, which are unto all people; he believed them, and was baptized into the name of Jesus, and given the name, "Anthony." Then, immediately, his soul yearned with sympathy towards his sister whom he left, a slave in the plantations; and he longed to make her a partaker of the same blessedness which he knew." (Source: The Bow in the Cloud, by Bonnie Barton, 1834. pages 2-4)

Shortly after this, the slave Anthony encountered a man named

Nicholas Von Zinzendorf, a landowner, and the leader of a group of 600 Christians, known as the Moravians, who were living on his land in Herrnhut. Anthony proclaimed his desire for the salvation of his sister, and the thousands of other slaves in the West Indies, and Zinzendorf was greatly moved. When he returned to Herrnhut, he shared with his fellow Moravians the testimony of Anthony, and his desire to see both his sister, and the other slaves, exposed to the gospel of Jesus. As Zinzendorf shared, Leonard Dober and his close friend Tobias Leopold were greatly stirred, and their hearts "burned within them to go forth."

That night, both young men stayed up late, praying, crying and pondering the possibility of going overseas to share the good news with the slaves there. The next morning, both were surprised and delighted to find that each had been stirred to the same call as they walked together through the forest. What happened next was quite amazing, and literally changed the course of missions history. As Dober and Leopold emerged from a forest trail, discussing their desire to take the gospel to the West Indies, they happened to pass by the home of ZInzendorf, who was standing at the door of his house discoursing with a visiting pastor named Reverend Shaeffer. Here again is Bonnie Barton, describing what happened next:

"As they [Dober and Leopold] passed towards their homes, Shaeffer turned to Zinzendorf and said, 'My dear friend, there are, amongst these brethren, messengers who will go forth to preach the gospel in the West Indies, Greenland, Lapland, and other heathen countries.'

This prophetic saying was the more remarkable, because no plan had yet been contemplated, nor was indeed likely to be undertaken, by these Christian exiles and immigrants...Nevertheless, the two friends, who had made up their minds for the service of the Lord, were encouraged by that saying to offer themselves up for the work...

In the course of a few weeks, Anthony himself arrived at Hermhut, and confirmed, at a public meeting there, all that he had stated at Copenhagen, respecting the wants and the willingness of his ignorant and oppressed countrymen in St. Thomas, to receive the gospel: but, he added, so long and so severely were they worked by their masters, that, unless those who went to preach to them would consent to become slaves themselves, and labour with the negroes in the plantations, they would have little opportunity of communicating divine instruction to them. This intelligence did not in the smallest degree daunt the devoted young men; they were both ready, not only to be bound, but to die for the Lord Jesus. Such indeed was the simplicity of purpose, singleness of heart, and strength of faith, by which they were actuated, that they were willing to make any sacrifice which might be required, if they could win but one soul to Christ, — nay, if they might but have the opportunity of carrying the news of salvation to Anthony's sister, — a poor despised female slave. " (Source: The Bow in the Cloud, by Bonnie Barton, 1834. pages 4-5) Note: the word 'negro,' is no longer in the common vernacular, and is considered offensive by many. Do keep in mind that this source is from 1834.

Shortly after this, in late 1732, Dober and David Nitschmann (who replaced Leopold for the first journey), traveled to Copenhagen, from where they hoped to obtain passage by boat to the Indies. The journey was not easy – they carried their luggage on their backs, had only 30 shillings between them, and traveled on foot 30 to 40 miles per day. From time to time, they would stop at the houses of Christian friends, and much of the time, they were met with discouragement when their mission was discovered. "Back! Back to Herrnhut, there is danger and death ahead," they were often told, according to J.E. Hutton's *A History of Moravian Missions*.

They did not turn back, however. They had put their hands to the plow, and they continued onward. At one point on their journey, according to Hutton, they did have an encouraging encounter with a fellow believer – the Countess of Stollberg. The Countess, upon discovering the mission of the Moravian brothers, asked young Dober how he felt about leaving behind his father and mother. She then brought him a box full of Scripture slivers – Bible verses written down on folded pieces of paper – and bade him draw one out. He randomly picked a Bible verse and she read it to him. It was Psalm 45:10-11, *"Pay attention and consider: forget your people and your father's house, and the king will desire your beauty. Bow down to him, for he is your lord."* The Countess was quite stirred by the text that Dober chose, and said to them, "Go then, and even if they kill you for the Savior's sake, He is worth it all." (Hutton, p. 23)

Upon arriving in Copenhagen shortly after this, the two brethren created quite a stir with their idea of sharing the gospel among the slaves. They were considered fools by both believers and nonbelievers; they were laughed at and even thought to be moonstruck. The directors of the Danish West Indian Company flatly denied them passage to the islands, saying, "It is no use taking artisans to St. Thomas as there is nothing for artisans to do, and you two men would never earn your living." (Hutton, p. 25)

Even their friend Anthony Ulrich, the former slave, turned his back on their mission. Upon seeing how much derision in Copenhagen was directed towards Nitschmann and Dober, he changed his original story, denounced the two Moravian brothers as fools, and declared that his family in the West Indies had no desire to hear the Gospel at all.

Dober and Nitschmann persisted, nonetheless. They were interviewed by the Danish King's chamberlain, who was concerned about how the two would sustain themselves while living in the West Indies. Dober and Nitschmann's reply was stunning, "As slaves among the slaves." The chamberlain was incredulous, retorting that no white men ever worked as slaves. Even then, Nitschmann and Dober persisted, causing the chamberlain to marvel at their resolve, "At this rate, you will stand your ground the wide world over!" (Hutton, 26)

Days of trouble followed this, and the Moravian brothers grew weary and discouraged. It was suggested they might consider joining the army of Denmark, which might somehow provide passage to the Indies; but this idea was soundly rejected by Dober and Nitschmann. After two weeks of delays, Dober was so discouraged that he suggested Nitschmann should consider returning to Herrnhut, an offer that was refused.

One day in the midst of waiting for breakthrough, both would-be missionaries were greatly encouraged by the prophetic declaration found in Numbers 23:19, "*God is not a man who lies, or a son of man who changes His mind. Does He speak and not act, or promise and not fulfill?*" They stood on this verse with renewed vigor and encouragement, and bit by bit, over the space of two months, the high and lofty of Denmark (who had initially scorned and mocked them) became their biggest supporters. They were given gifts of money and tribute by princes, princesses and even the king's chamberlain, and had passage arranged to the West Indies by the king's cup-bearer.

The journey to the West Indies would be difficult. The captain of their ship was an atheist, and nobody aboard the ship were Christians. Initially, Dober and Nitschmann were treated roughly by the sailors, but they returned such treatment with kindness, patience and resolve, and eventually even the hardened captain was won over by their character.

Upon arrival on Saint Thomas, there is some debate about whether or not Dober and Nitschmann actually sold themselves into slavery, or whether they worked their trades (carpentry and pottery-making) among the slaves as freemen, but either way, they labored patiently in the West Indies for years - working hard and sharing the gospel among the slave laborers. Their message to the slaves was proclaimed passionately and relationally, as the Moravian brothers toiled among and alongside the slaves of the Indies. Though Dober and Nitschmann struggled to master the Creole language of the slaves, they did their best to proclaim that Christ had died for blacks as well as for whites. Initially, the slaves "clapped their hands for joy." upon hearing the message. According to Dober, "they felt the truth, rather than fully understood it," due to the language difficulties, but Dober and Nitschmann persisted in their mission to learn the Creole language better and to understand the native people of the islands.

The greatest hindrance to the gospel in the West Indies was hypocrisy. The white planters and slave owners of the area were "Christian," at least in the way they identified themselves. In practice and matters of the heart, however, they were hardly followers of Christ. In their understanding of religion, as long as they didn't engage in any serious Sabbath day work, God was pleased with them. They absolutely forbid the slaves of their plantations to have religious services, or worship God at all. They told them that blacks were created by the Devil, and that Jesus had died only for white people. (Hutton, p. 33) Nitschmann and Dober persisted in sharing the gospel to the slaves despite all of this.

It was difficult. Shortly after arrival, Nitschmann was recalled to Moravia leaving Dober alone and leading him to become so destitute that he even attempted to work for the black slaves for his sustenance. Still, he persisted in the gospel mission through untold hardships. There were rebellions on the island, mass suicides (of 300 slaves at once!), murders, and health problems. However, more Moravian brothers were sent into the mission field, and they too persisted in sharing the good news that Jesus had died and risen equally for white and black persons. The trials faced by those Moravian missionaries are numerous enough, and severe enough, to fill another book, but still they persisted.

Ultimately, this incarnational mission was an unqualified success. Through the efforts of Dober and Nitschmann, and many of the other Moravian brethren that came after them, over 13,000 West Indies slave laborers were baptized and converted. Mission churches were founded in Antigua, St. Thomas, Barbados, St. Kitts, Jamaica and St. Croix. It would be 50 years before any other church or denomination sent any sort of ministry outreach to the slaves of the West Indies.

What does this story have to do with racism and race relations? Simply this: We need more Dobers, Leopolds and Nitschmanns in the Body of Christ today. They did not let whatever privilege they might have been accorded due to the color of their skin keep them from following Christ to take the gospel to those in desperate need. The did not reckon themselves as too lofty to give up all they had to carry the gospel to the least of these. They did not let the slaves' understandable distrust of white people, nor their resistance to the biblical message stop them. They staked their lives on the twin truths of Luke 19:10 ("*For the Son of Man has come to seek and to save the lost.*") and Acts 10:28 ("*Peter said to them, "You know it's forbidden for a Jewish man to associate with or visit a foreigner. But God has shown me that I must not call any person common or unclean."*") And they left whatever safety they had to sacrificially carry the good news of Jesus to those in the world of a different language, tribe, tongue and hemisphere. And God blessed that mission beyond their wildest imaginings.

I love how Dr. David Eung-Yul Ryoo, professor at Chongshin Theological Seminary in South Korea, describes the qualifications that Zinzendorf looked for in missionaries like Dober and Nitschmann.

Leonard Dober, a potter, and David Nitschmann, a carpenter, were the first two missionaries to the West Indies, and the next two missionaries to Greenland were gravediggers. Like the apostles in the early church, they were unlearned and ignorant men; and like them, they were despised by the cultured people of their day. But they were men of passion and piety. What they lacked in knowledge from theological education they made up in zeal for Christ and love for lost souls. Zinzendorf did not really pay much attention to the educational qualifications of the missionaries. He emphasized passion and love for Jesus more than formal education. This attitude was influential for a long time in the Moravian Church. The synods of 1818 and 1825 declined the establishment of a college for missionary training.

Their decision does not mean that they ignored the need of theological education, but rather that they put more emphasis on the work of the Holy Spirit and the commitment of the missionaries. The great fruit of the Moravians shows that the best missionaries are those equipped with the power of the Holy Spirit and with a burning heart for the unreached. Zinzendorf laid emphasis not only upon the spiritual qualifications for a missionary, but he also stressed that they should be men of character. As self supporting lay persons, the Moravian missionaries worked with the natives, witnessing their faith not only by their words but also by their exemplary lives. (Source: The Moravian Mission's Strategy: Christ-Centered, Spirit-Driven and Mission-Minded, by David Eung-Yl Ryoo. 2008, p. 46) online plain text editor. Enter or paste your text here. To download and save it, click on the button below.

It would seem that Dr. David Platt, president of the Southern Baptist International Mission Board, is adopting a very Moravian-like strategy going forward, slightly de-emphasizing seminary education, while focusing more on sending self-supporting lay people with extraordinary character and zeal. I suspect that wonderful fruit will come out of that effort.

3

Jesus said, "ONE!"

I pray not only for these, but also for those who believe in Me through their message. 21 May they all be one, as You, Father, are in Me and I am in You.May they also be one in Us, so the world may believe You sent Me. 22 I have given them the glory You have given Me. May they be one as We are one. 23 I am in them and You are in Me. May they be made completely one, so the world may know You have sent Me and have loved them as You have loved Me. – Jesus, John 17:20-23

John 17 – Jesus praying before His arrest and crucifixion.

What we often call "The Lord's Prayer," found in Matthew 6, might be more properly deemed "The Model Prayer," as it is focused on *teaching* Jesus' followers how to pray, but was not necessarily a prayer that Jesus actually prayed. Perhaps a more apt "Lord's Prayer," is found in John 17, which contains a roughly 600 word prayer of Jesus. This prayer, offered up to God immediately before Jesus was arrested, is incredibly significant. It represents the Son of God praying to God the Father, right before the two most momentous events in human history, the crucifixion and the resurrection. Jesus knows He is about to be separated from His disciples for a time, and knows that things will be permanently changed after His resurrection. Thus, He prays passionately and deeply for His disciples AND for those that would ultimately believe in Jesus through their testimony.

Strikingly, John 17 might just be the prayer that Jesus prayed with such intensity that his sweat became like great drops of blood. (Luke

22:44) Even MORE striking than that, at least to me, is that Jesus was praying for His followers in 2017, and we know what He prayed for us. Jesus' prayer in John 17 is a very, very clear indication of His will for believers in 2017. FOUR times in that short section of Jesus' prayer (vss 20-23), Jesus prays for His future followers to be ONE. FOUR TIMES. Let that sink in...of all of the things that Jesus could pray for believers in 2017, He prayed FOUR times for His followers to be ONE.

> *I pray not only for these, but also for those who believe in Me through their message. 21 May they all be one, as You, Father, are in Me and I am in You. May they also be one in Us, so the world may believe You sent Me. 22 I have given them the glory You have given Me. May they be one as We are one. 23 I am in them and You are in Me. May they be made completely one, so the world may know You have sent Me and have loved them as You have loved Me. (John 17:20-23)*

The oneness that is put forward in the prayer of Jesus wages war against racism, racial preferences, segregated Sunday mornings and ANY sort of race-based bias or separation. It wars against the slavery-based racism of the American South in 1800s. It wars against the separate but equal provisions made in this country in the 1950s. It wars against segregation in the 1960s, white flight in the 1970s-80s and separated places of worship in the 1990s and 2000s. It is a bracing splash of cold water in the face for all who think that Christians with different skin color should be anything but in tight unity.

What sort of tight unity should Christians enjoy and seek? The kind of deep unity that is characterized and illustrated by the relationship that the Son has with the Father. Pause and think about THAT relationship. The relationship between God the Father, God the Son, and God the Holy Spirit, as is manifested in the Trinity, is the very closest, deepest and tightest relationship possible in all existence.

Therefore, the fact that Jesus prayed that His followers – red, yellow, white, black – would be one, as He and the Father are one, is one of the most profound things in the Bible. And far too often we Christians, particularly American Christians, have ignored this truth and this profound prayer of our Lord and Master.

The Summer of 2017 (when this book was written) has been a profound time of racial unrest in most Western countries. In the United States, the news is constantly reporting on one racially tinged conflict after another, seemingly a new one every day. Whether it be related to white supremacists marching, minorities being shot by law enforcement, the destruction of Confederate monuments, or the the rise of far right and far left agitation groups, racial tensions that are already simmering, seem to be ready to boil over in this country. When a reasonable and honorable sitting United States Senator like Ben Sasse posts a warning that violence might be coming, I sit up and take notice.

Over the last week, many Nebraskans have told me some version of this: "There are lots of us here who are scared about where the country is headed. I think more violence is inevitable." That much seems obvious....Tragically, there are some who want violence. Most Americans see the images from Charlottesville and our hearts break. We yearn for leaders, who raise high the exceptional American Idea of universal human dignity. But there are others who want to see these divisions exacerbated — not only the extremists on the ground but also some cable news executives who jump at division and know that what's bad for America is good for ratings....It feels like violence is coming. I'm not sure if this moment is like the summer of '67 or not. But it might be. Before that violence strikes again, it's up to us to reaffirm that exceptional American Creed again today, with our neighbors, and in our kids' hearts. (Source: The official Facebook page of Senator Ben Sasse facebook.com/SenatorSasse August 18, 2017 Title: "The Next Charlottesville")

I hope the church is taking notice too. These are perilous times, and it is incredibly tricky knowing how to properly speak to issues of race right now. People are far too easily offended, and people are far too quick to say offensive things. This is an incredible moment of opportunity for all who are followers of Jesus Christ. An opportunity to be the light that He has called His followers to be, and to be savory salt to a confused, angry, and hurting world. This is not the time to sit on the sideline and watch. This is not the time to angrily seek to advance our own political or personal agendas either. This is the time to "plead on Christ's behalf," that people would "*be reconciled to God.*" (2nd Corinthians 5:20) This is a time to "*seek peace and pursue it,*" (1 Peter 3:11) And this is a time to obey and pray, in accord with the prayers of Jesus, that we would be ONE.

4

Does the Bible Condone Racism?

11 In Christ there is not Greek and Jew, circumcision and uncir-
cumcision, barbarian, Scythian, slave and free; but Christ is all
and in all. 12 Therefore, God's chosen ones, holy and loved, put on
heartfelt compassion, kindness, humility, gentleness, and patience,
13 accepting one another and forgiving one another if anyone has
a complaint against another. Just as the Lord has forgiven you, so
you must also forgive. 14 Above all, put on love—the perfect bond
of unity. 15 And let the peace of the Messiah, to which you were
also called in one body, control your hearts. Be thankful.
The Apostle Paul, Colossians 3:11‒15

[Image of text fragments including: "s of", "be it", "ntel-", "ht is", "rced", "year.", "this", "increased", "and which should be", "relate to this.", "Racism: the definition", "and different races to", "discrimination and pre", "scribed the meaning", "that the basis o"]

"The Word [Jesus} shows His compassion and His denial of all respect of persons by all the saints, He enlightens them and adapts them to that which is advantageous for us, like a skillful physician, understanding the weakness of men. And the ignorant He loves to teach, and the erring He turns again to His own true way. And by those who live by faith He is easily found; and to those of pure eye and holy heart, who desire to knock at the door, He opens immediately. For He casts away none of His servants as unworthy of the divine mysteries. He does not esteem the rich man more highly than the poor, nor does He despise the poor man for his poverty. He does not disdain the barbarian, nor does He set the eunuch aside as no man.7 He does not hate the female on account of the woman's act of disobedience in the beginning, nor does He reject the male on account of the man's transgression. But He seeks all, and desires to save all, wishing to make all the children of God, and calling all the saints unto one perfect man. For there is also one Son of God, by whom we too, receiving *the regeneration through the Holy Spirit, desire to come all unto one perfect and heavenly man." Hippolytus of Rome, 200 AD, "Treatise on Christ and Antichrist," in Fathers of the Third Century: Hippolytus, Cyprian, Novatian. (Buffalo, NY: Christian Literature Company, 1886), 205.)*

But they do not represent any as entering upon that way except boys and young men; for this reason, that the arts are learned at these ages. We, on the other hand, lead those of each sex, every age and race, into this heavenly path, because God, who is the guide of that way, denies immortality to no human being. (Source: Lactantius, circa 290 AD "The Divine Institutes," in Fathers of the Third and Fourth Centuries: vol. 7, The Ante-Nicene Fathers (Buffalo, NY: Christian Literature Company, 1886), 165.)

"The Bible is racist," opine thousands of internet commenters, in every nook and cranny of the internet. On sites like Reddit (where I'm a 9 year member), one frequently comes across charges like this one, from user Minorityvote, "The bible is racist, sexist, and homophobic, when you try and change that to try and make it fit with the modern age, it stops being the Bible." Commenters like Kirk on Discovery magazine make charges like this with regularity, "Most people who consider themselves religious disregard the racist elements in the Bible and other religious texts." Even on Youtube (especially on Youtube!), one is likely to find the charge that the Bible is racist – there are almost 500 videos devoted to this 'fact,' some of whom are pro-racism, and others anti-racism.

Much contemporary racism is rooted in Christianity. Unfortunately, the Bible is not very helpful when it comes to race issues. Many have found within its pages justifications for slavery, abuse of African-Americans and segregation. Unfortunately, the divisions between the races are exacerbated, not diminished, by Christianity... The single greatest humiliation of American Christianity is its long endorsement of slavery and even longer endorsement of racism — a dark cloud still clearly visible at eleven o'clock on Sunday mornings — a cloud that mocks the vision of Martin Luther King and the leaders of the civil rights movement. (Source: Karl Gilberson, Huffington Post www.huffingtonpost.com/karl-giberson-phd the-biblical-roots-of-racism_b_7649390.html)

Could such a charge be true? Are there racist elements in the teachings of the Bible? In the next chapter, we will survey 20 Bible passages, composed of hundreds of verses, which convincingly show that the Bible is not even remotely a racist book, but is rather an anti-racist document that unmistakably demonstrates the folly of white supremacy and every other racial fallacy circling the globe during modern times.

This is a time to present the Bible's strong and clear teachings about the sin of racism and of the idolatry of blood and country. In Acts 17:26, in the midst of an evangelistic lecture to secular, pagan philosophers, Paul makes the case that God created all the races "from one man." Paul's Greek listeners saw other races as barbarian, but against such views of racial superiority Paul makes the case that all races have the same Creator and are of one stock. Since all are made in God's image, every human life is of infinite and equal value (Gen. 9:5–6).
When Jonah puts the national interests of Israel ahead of the spiritual good of the racially "other" pagan city of Nineveh, he is roundly condemned by God (Jonah 4:1–11). One main

effect of the gospel is to shatter the racial barriers that separate people (Gal. 3:28; Eph. 2:14–18), so it is an egregious sin to do anything to support those barriers. When Peter sought to do so, Paul reprimanded him for losing his grasp on the gospel (Gal. 2:14). (Writer and pastor Timothy Keller, responding to the Charlottesville white supremacist's march of August, 2017. Source: www.thegospelcoalition.org

/article/race-the-gospel-and-the-moment)

5

20 Foundational Bible Passages on Racism

God is not asking black to be white, or white to be black. He's asking both to be biblical. If I say I am a Black Christian and somebody else says that they're a White Christian, what they've done is made black or white an adjective...Your faith should always be in the adjectival position, so that you're always adjusting the noun of your culture to the objective of your faith. In other works, you're bringing who you are – your history, your background, and your culture to look like the adjectival description of what you say you believe about God and Jesus Christ. (Source: Tony Evans in Tony Evans' Book of Illustrations, 2000, p. 242)

Dr. Tony Evans Preaching

The Bible discusses race and issues related to racism, nationality, favoritism and unity quite frequently. Finding skin color references in the Bible is somewhat difficult, however. Esau is described in Genesis 25 as having reddish skin. The wife of Solomon, spoken of in the Bible's great love poem, describes herself as dark-skinned in Song of Solomon 1:5. In Acts 13:1, there is a deacon of the church named Simeon who had the nickname of "Niger/black," possibly because he was a dark-skinned man.

The Bible does mention white skin with a small degree of regularity, but don't get too excited if you are of the white-supremacist bent. In literally *every* situation in the Bible where white skin is mentioned, the context is DISEASE. Such an example is found in Exodus 4:7 when, as a sign, Moses puts his hand in his cloak and draws it out diseased, as "white as snow." Or Leviticus 13: which discusses white skin in terms of a disgusting skin disease. There's also Miriam's punishment for rebellion in Numbers 12:10, which turns her skin white, and Naaman's white as snow skin in 2 Kings 5, that signified the presence of disease on him. The only other possible appearance of white skin in the Bible is a very tenuous one. The description of Israel in Lamentations 4:7 says that, prior to sinning, they were "whiter than milk." If you keep reading, however, it also says they were "redder than coral," and looked like sapphires, which are generally blue. One would be more justified in thinking that Jeremiah, the writer of Lamentations, meant to communicate that the red, white and blue Israelites were actually Americans, than that he meant to communicate that they were lily white-skinned. (Jeremiah was, quite clearly, speaking in metaphor here.)

Does this mean that God doesn't like white-skinned people? Of course not...but it does indubitably demonstrate that the Bible contains zero bias in favor of white-skinned people. Past assertions of slave-owners and slave traders that Jesus only died for white people find no basis in the Bible whatsoever.

What we do find throughout the Bible is a consistent call for unity and oneness in Christ. The following 25 Bible passages are meant to present a large sample of the biblical teaching on race and racism. The passages do not represent a totality of biblical teaching on the subject, but they do give a very solid beginning overview. With each passage, I will endeavor to include a sufficient context so as to clearly present the overall intention of the passage. You will note, for reasons that will be more fully discussed in chapter 6, that I am including a significantly larger amount of New Testament verses than Old Testament. This chapter and chapter 7 are the most important and foundational chapters of this book. The passages below outline clearly what the Bible has to communicate on the issues of race and racism. Unless otherwise noted, each passage is from the Holman Christian Standard Translation.

1. Genesis 1:27 So God created man in His own image; He created him in the image of God; He created them male and female.

One of the great foundational truths of the Bible - that ALL men and women are created in the Imago Dei, the Image of God – is THE great foundational truth of this book. Undeniably, unquestionably, and with unmistakable clarity, the Bible declares that EVERY person, EVERY skin color, EVERY race, EVERY tribe, EVERY tongue – ALL are made in the Image of God. There is no significant modifier to that truth found anywhere in the entire Bible. There is not even a hint that one skin color or one race or even one nationality is made LESS in the Image of God than any other skin color, race or nationality. All races are equally created in the Image of God. This one fact alone, properly understood, SHOULD be enough to dispel any racist ideals and to disabuse proud members of ANY race that their race is somehow superior.

Compare the truths of Genesis 1:27 (above) and Acts 10, 17, etc, listed below, with this passage from a 1914 Darwinian science textbook.

> *The Races of man.* – – – *At the present time there exist upon the earth five races or varieties of man, each very different from the other in instincts, social customs, and, to an extent, in structure. These are the Ethiopian or negro type, originating in Africa; the Malay or brown race, from the islands of the Pacific; the American Indian; the Mongolian or yellow race, including the natives of China, Japan, and the Eskimos; and finally,* **the highest type of all, the Caucasions,** *represented by the civilized white inhabitants of Europe and America. (Source: A Civic Biology, by George Hunter. 1914. This science textbook, which covers a wide variety of topics including eugenics, was the science curriculum at the center of the 1925 Scopes Monkey Trial, in which a substitute teacher was accused of teaching evolution (in violation of Tennessee law) via this textbook.)*

Scientific Racism, as the above is an example of, was prevalent for many years in scientific literature, and is found to penetrate some of the works of Darwin, including *The Descent of Man.* Many people today rightly point out that there were Christian clergy that were vocal supporters of race-based slavery in Europe and the United States in prior centuries. Most, however, are less aware of the many science books and scientists, like the above, that were also unabashed promoters of racism during this time.

Racism in the 1800s was not merely limited to scientists and preachers. At the time of the speech below, Alexander Stephens was the first vice-president of the Confederacy, and a former U.S. Senator from the state of Georgia. He would go on to become the 50th governor of Georgia in the 1880s. In railing against the United States, the Declaration of Independence AND clear biblical truth, Stevens gave a famous speech (known as The Cornerstone Speech) prior to the beginning of the Civil War. In that speech, he unapologetically made the case that the preservation of the African slavery was at the center of the southern decision to secede, and at the center of the coming armed conflict. Further, he claimed that the white man's 'right' to hold African slaves was directly from Providence.

> "The new [Confederate] Constitution has put at rest forever all the agitating questions relating to our peculiar institutions—African slavery as it exists among us—the proper status of the negro in our form of civilization. This was the immediate cause of the late rupture and present revolution [the Civil War]. Jefferson, in his forecast, had anticipated this, as the "rock upon which the old Union would split." He was right...
> The prevailing ideas entertained by him and most of the leading statesmen at the time of the formation of the old Constitution were, that the enslavement of the African was in violation of the laws of nature; that it was wrong in principle, socially, morally and politically. It was an evil they knew not well how to deal with; but the general opinion of the men of that day was, that, somehow or other, in the order of Providence, the institution would be evanescent and pass away...

Those ideas, however, were fundamentally wrong. They rested upon the assumption of the equality of races. This was an error. It was a sandy foundation, and the idea of a Government built upon it—when the "storm came and the wind blew, it fell." Our new government is founded upon exactly the opposite idea; its foundations are laid, its cornerstone rests, upon the great truth that the negro is not equal to the white man; that slavery — subordination to the superior race — is his natural and normal condition. This, our new government, is the first, in the history of the world, based upon this great physical, philosophical, and moral truth. It is the first government ever instituted upon the principles in strict conformity to nature, and the ordination of Providence." (Source: Cornerstone Speech in Savannah, Georgia on March 21, 1861.)

Observe well that Stevens declares – without using any Scripture whatsoever – that whites in America were superior (and blacks inferior) by the ordering of Providence. He completely ignores Genesis 1:27, that all men were made in the image of God.

Further note, with appropriate indignation, that Steven's monstrous assertions are contradicted and abominated by other Scriptures also. As a white, southern, Alabama-born preacher, and Christian writer, it fills me with a special kind of indignation that our Confederate forebears used Scripture to justify race-based slavery, abuse, racism and secession. Fools.

2. Acts 17:26 From one man He has made every nationality to live over the whole earth and has determined their appointed times and the boundaries of where they live.

Acts 17:26 represents another great foundational truth of the Bible, boiled down to one sentence. All humans spring from one man, Adam, and thus all humans have common ancestry. This ideal forms a significant pillar of the Bible's teaching on race, and it completely repudiates any sort of racist ideology that God created different races for different purposes. In commenting on this passage, John Piper writes:

First, notice that God is the MAKER of ethnic groups. "God made from one every nation." Ethnic groups do not just come about by random genetic change. They come about by God's design and purpose. The text says plainly, "GOD made every ethnos."

Second, notice that God made all the ethnic groups from one human ancestor. Paul says, "He made FROM ONE every ethnos." This has a special wallop when you ponder why he chose to say just this to these Athenians on the Areopagus. The Athenians were fond of boasting that they were autochthones, which means that they sprang from their native soil and were not immigrants from some other place or people group. (See Lenski and Bruce, ad. loc.) Paul chooses to confront this ethnic pride head on. God made all the ethnic groups—Athenians and Barbarians—and he made them out of one common stock. So you Athenians are cut from the same cloth as those despised Barbarians and Scythians. Source: http://www.desiringgod.org/messages/racial-reconciliation

*3. Acts 10: 9 **The next day, as they were traveling and nearing the city, Peter went up to pray on the housetop about noon. 10 Then he became hungry and wanted to eat, but while they were preparing something, he went into a visionary state. 11 He*** *saw heaven opened and an object that resembled a large sheet coming down, being lowered by its four corners to the earth. 12 In it were all the four-footed animals and reptiles of the earth, and the birds of the sky. 13 Then a voice said to him, "Get up, Peter; kill and eat!" 14 "No, Lord!" Peter said. "For I have never eaten anything common and ritually unclean!" 15 Again, a second time, a voice said to him, "What God has made clean, you must not call common." 16 This happened three times, and then the object was taken up into heaven.*

In Acts 10, Peter has a dream in which God shows him a bunch of (formerly) unclean animals, and bids him to eat them. Initially Peter refuses, but God tells him that he must no longer call "common/un-clean," what God has made clean. The implications of this direct communication from God are understood by Peter immediately to be far more comprehensive then merely affecting dietary laws. Upon waking up, Peter finds that some foreigners have come to his house to collect Peter and bring him to their leader Cornelius, a Roman centurion. Peter goes without hesitation (though according to some forms of the Jewish oral law, Peter shouldn't have). Upon arrival, something remarkable happens, which makes up the bulk of passage #4.

4. Acts 10:28-46 Peter said to them, "You know it's forbidden for a Jewish man to associate with or visit a foreigner. But God has shown me that I must not call any person common or unclean... 34 Then Peter began to speak: "Now I really understand that God doesn't show favoritism, 35 but in every nation the person who fears Him and does righteousness is acceptable to Him. 36 He sent the message to the Israelites, proclaiming the good news of peace through Jesus Christ—He is Lord of all. 37 You know the events that took place throughout Judea, beginning from Galilee after the baptism that John preached: 38 how God anointed Jesus of

Nazareth with the Holy Spirit and with power, and how He went about doing good and healing all who were under the tyranny of the Devil, because God was with Him. 39 We ourselves are witnesses of everything He did in both the Judean country and in Jerusalem, yet they killed Him by hanging Him on a tree. 40 God raised up this man on the third day and permitted Him to be seen, 41 not by all the people, but by us, witnesses appointed beforehand by God, who ate and drank with Him after He rose from the dead. 42 He commanded us to preach to the people and to solemnly testify that He is the One appointed by God to be the Judge of the living and the dead. 43 All the prophets testify about Him that through His name everyone who believes in Him will receive forgiveness of sins."

44 While Peter was still speaking these words, the Holy Spirit came down on all those who heard the message. 45 The circumcised believers who had come with Peter were astounded because the gift of the Holy Spirit had been poured out on the Gentiles also. 46 For they heard them speaking in other languages and declaring the greatness of God.

Without being a Jewish person, it is very difficult to understand just how monumental this happening was in the life of Peter, and the life of the early church. The Jews were not a people who associated with other nationalities and races very frequently, in large part because God had warned them after the Exodus to not intermarry with those who did not worship Him. It would seem that some of the Jewish people of the first century, and the rabbis who wrote the Mishnah, interpreted God's commands in the direction of race and ethnicity, rather than understanding them to be based on worship. More on this dynamic shortly.

5. *Acts 15:7-11 After there had been much debate, Peter stood up and said to them: "Brothers, you are aware that in the early*

days God made a choice among you, that by my mouth the Gentiles would hear the gospel message and believe. 8 And God, who knows the heart, testified to them by giving the Holy Spirit, just as He also did to us. 9 He made no distinction between us and them, cleansing their hearts by faith. 10 Now then, why are you testing God by putting a yoke on the disciples' necks that neither our ancestors nor we have been able to bear? 11 On the contrary, we believe we are saved through the grace of the Lord Jesus in the same way they are."

In Acts 15, Peter recounts how God gloriously saved the Gentiles in Cornelius' house as they heard the gospel of Jesus being proclaimed. while describing that episode, Peter here makes two declarations on race that should be noted. 1. God makes NO distinction between the Jews and other races. 2. Other races and nationalities are saved by grace through faith in the exact same way that the early Jewish disciples were.

*6. Revelation 7:9-10 9 **After this I looked, and there was a vast multitude from every nation, tribe, people, and language, which no one could number, standing before the throne and before the Lamb. They were robed in white with palm branches in their hands. 10 And they cried out in a loud voice: "Salvation belongs to our God, who is seated on the throne, and to the Lamb!"***

How difficult such a passage must be to somebody who is a white, black, yellow or red supremacist?! According to the Revelation of John, Heaven is composed of "*a vast multitude from EVERY nation, tribe, people and language.*" And they are all evenly spread around God's throne! Passages like this obliterate racist ideals and racist principles in the light of truth, and demonstrate the completely illogical nature of one somehow being a 'Christian' racist.

THE BIBLE AND RACISM

7. Acts 2:5-11 5 There were Jews living in Jerusalem, devout men from every nation under heaven. 6 When this sound occurred, a crowd came together and was confused because each one heard them speaking in his own language. 7 And they were astounded and amazed, saying, "Look, aren't all these who are speaking Galileans? 8 How is it that each of us can hear in our own native language? 9 Parthians, Medes, Elamites; those who live in Mesopotamia, in Judea and Cappadocia, Pontus and Asia, 10 Phrygia and Pamphylia, Egypt and the parts of Libya near Cyrene; visitors from Rome, both Jews and proselytes, 11 Cretans and Arabs—we hear them speaking the magnificent acts of God in our own languages."

The significance of Acts 2, and that long list of nationalities found in verses 9-11, cannot be understated! In Luke 24, Jesus had instructed His disciples and followers to "wait in Jerusalem until they were clothed with power from on high." Acts Chapter 2 records that clothing in power and the birth of the church, and I note with joy that at least 17 different ethnic groups heard the wonders of the good news of Jesus (in their own language!) on the day that Jesus first clothed His disciples with the power and presence of the Holy Spirit. The end result of Acts 2 was that the church, the assembly of Jesus, was born, and it was a mixed-race entity from the very beginning, by sovereign plan and design of God.

8. Luke 2:28-32 28 Simeon took Him up in his arms, praised God, and said:
29 Now, Master, You can dismiss Your slave in peace, as You promised.
30 For my eyes have seen Your salvation. 31 You have prepared it in the presence of all peoples— 32 a light for revelation to the Gentiles and glory to Your people Israel.

Luke 2 records the prophetic pronouncements of Simeon, an old prophet who was waiting in the temple to see the Messiah. He proclaimed the will of God over baby Jesus: that He would be glory for the people of Israel AND a light for revelation to the Gentiles – ALL of the other nations.

> *9. Acts 13:46-49* **Then Paul and Barnabas boldly said: "It was** **necessary that God's message be spoken to you first. But since** **you reject it and consider yourselves unworthy of eternal life,** **we now turn to the Gentiles! 47 For this is what the Lord has** **commanded us: I have made you a light for the Gentiles to bring** **salvation to the ends of the earth." 48 When the Gentiles heard** **this, they rejoiced and glorified the message of the Lord, and** **all who had been appointed to eternal life believed. 49 So the** **message of the Lord spread through the whole region.**

When Paul and Barnabas were in Pisidian Antioch, they went to the Jewish synagogue there for a Sabbath service. While there, they were invited to speak, and Paul spoke about Jesus, causing a great uproar among the Jews present, who rejected Paul's message. This incident caused a tremendous change in Paul's evangelism, as he adjusted his strategy to preach much more frequently to those of other nations after this. We see here the scriptural rationale for such a decision: Jesus was a light to the Gentiles, a light to other nations.

> *10. Romans 2:6-11* **He will repay each one according to his works:** **7 eternal life to those who by persistence in doing good seek** **glory, honor, and immortality; 8 but wrath and indignation to** **those who are self-seeking and disobey the truth but are obeying** **unrighteousness; 9 affliction and distress for every human being** **who does evil, first to the Jew, and also to the Greek; 10 but glory,** **honor, and peace for everyone who does what is good, first to the** **Jew, and also to the Greek. 11 There is no favoritism with God.**

11. James 2: 1-9 _My brothers, do not show favoritism as you hold on to the faith in our glorious Lord Jesus Christ. 2 For example, a man comes into your meeting wearing a gold ring and dressed in fine clothes, and a poor man dressed in dirty clothes also comes in. 3 If you look with favor on the man wearing the fine clothes and say, "Sit here in a good place," and yet you say to the poor man, "Stand over there," or, "Sit here on the floor by my footstool," 4 haven't you discriminated among yourselves and become judges with evil thoughts?5 Listen, my dear brothers: Didn't God choose the poor in this world to be rich in faith and heirs of the kingdom that He has promised to those who love Him? 6 Yet you dishonored that poor man. Don't the rich oppress you and drag you into the courts? 7 Don't they blaspheme the noble name that was pronounced over you at your baptism? 8 Indeed, if you keep the royal law prescribed in the Scripture, Love your neighbor as yourself, you are doing well. 9 But if you show favoritism, you commit sin and are convicted by the law as transgressors._

Paul and James both declare an important truth for Christians: There is simply NO room for any sort of favoritism among Christians. Not racial favoritism, not economic favoritism, not nationality based favoritism. Instead of favoritism, the royal law of Jesus dictates that Christians should love their neighbors as their selves.

12. *Galatians 3:26-29 For you are all sons of God through faith in Christ Jesus. For as many of you as have been baptized into Christ have put on Christ like a garment. 28 There is no Jew or Greek, slave or free, male or female; for you are all one in Christ Jesus. 29 And if you belong to Christ, then you are Abraham's seed, heirs according to the promise.*

ALL have equal value and worth in Christ. All are co-heirs with Christ of the glories of the coming age. In a sermon from 2011, David Platt offers a good explanation of this passage:

Paul says that "in Christ there is neither Jew nor Greek, slave nor free, male nor female, for you are all one in Christ Jesus." So, yes, we have differences, but we all have equal dignity before God and equal position in Christ. It's the basis upon which James, in James 2, says, "Do not show favoritism." We all have equal dignity before God. So, this is one of those areas where the Bible may not be prohibiting, expressly, all forms of slavery, but it is absolutely ripping apart the foundation of slavery that says one person has more dignity before God than another, that one person has more value than another, and any place where that is happening, including in slavery, is condemned by God in His Word. So, first, we all have equal dignity before God. David Platt, "What about Slavery, Paul?," in David Platt Sermon Archive (Birmingham, AL: David Platt, 2011), 3174. Note: We will cover the thorny issue of slavery and the Bible in upcoming chapters.

13. Deuteronomy 1:17 AND Deuteronomy 10:17 **Do not show partiality when deciding a case; listen to small and great alike. Do not be intimidated by anyone, for judgment belongs to God. Bring me any case too difficult for you, and I will hear it....For the Lord your God is the God of gods and Lord of lords, the great, mighty, and awesome God, showing no partiality and taking no bribe.** *It should be noted that it was said of Jesus also that He did not show partiality. (In Mark 12, Matthew 22 and Luke 20)*

Because God does not show partiality or favoritism, then Christians should not do so either.

14. Revelation 5:8-10 **When He took the scroll, the four living creatures and the 24 elders fell down before the Lamb. Each one had a harp and gold bowls filled with incense, which are the prayers of the saints. 9 And they sang a new song: You are worthy to take the scroll and to open its seals, because You were slaughtered, and You redeemed people for God by Your blood** *from every tribe and language and people and nation. 10 You made them a kingdom and priests to our God, and they will reign on the earth.*

Once again we see the declaration that the people of Jesus who will spend eternity together are taken out of every tribe, tongue, people and nation. ALL skin colors and ALL different types of people are represented. ALL of these races and peoples are being forged by Jesus into a "kingdom and priests" to God. Once again – the equality of ALL races, ALL skin colors ALL languages, and ALL nationalities is abundantly demonstrated here.

> *15. 1st Samuel 16:7 But the Lord said to Samuel, "Do not look at his appearance or his stature, because I have rejected him. Man does not see what the Lord sees, for man sees what is visible, but the Lord sees the heart."*

In this passage, God has called His prophet Samuel to go and anoint King Saul's successor as the next king of Israel. Upon arriving at the house of Jesse, Samuel is presented with Jesse's son Eliab, who was apparently a very impressive and imposing looking man. Immediately, Samuel assumes that it is Eliab that is to be anointed king, but God rebukes him for his errant thought with the profound truth that God is not concerned with what is visible about a person, but what makes up his innermost being. One of the first things most people notice about other people is their appearance, size, skin color, level of beauty, etc. Humans consider this very important, but notice the dismissive air in God's tone here – it is ungodly, by definition, to judge people by skin color, nationality, etc. God looks on the INSIDE. Skin and signs of race are on the OUTSIDE.

> *16. Luke 16:15 And He told them: "You are the ones who justify yourselves in the sight of others, but God knows your hearts. For*

what is highly admired by people is revolting in God's sight."

Luke 16:15 goes hand-in-hand with 1 Samuel 16:7, and is simply yet another strong indicator that the visible way that we make judgments is contrary to God's way of making judgments about people. God looks on hearts and thoughts and the inside.

> 17. *Mark 11:17 (and Isaiah 56:7)* **Then He began to teach them: "Is it not written, My house will be called a house of prayer for all nations? But you have made it a den of thieves!"**

Both the Old Testament and New Testament's declare that God's temple – His house is ultimately meant to be a house of prayer and worship for **ALL nations,** not merely the Jews.

> 18. *Romans 10:11-13* **Now the Scripture says, Everyone who believes on Him will not be put to shame, 12 for there is no distinction between Jew and Greek, since the same Lord of all is rich to all who call on Him. 13 For everyone who calls on the name of the Lord will be saved.**

This is one of my favorite Bible passages of all the ones listed here. There is **NO DISTINCTION** between Jew and Greek. I'm not typing those words in bold because I'm angry, but because I am joyful and excited! I've never understand antisemitism, especially among people that claimed to be Christian. Jesus was a Jew. Paul was a Jew. All of the great heroes of the Bible were Jews! If I could choose my race, which I can't, I would be Jewish – what a privilege that would be! In the long run, however, it does NOT matter. Why not? Because there is NO DISTINCTION between Jews and Greeks/Gentiles/Other nations! God is RICH to ALL who would call on Him, no matter their race, nor sex, nor wealth level, nor physical beauty, not popularity or whatever. This is a truth we should all rejoice in.

19. Revelation 14:6-7 Then I saw another angel flying high overhead, having the eternal gospel to announce to the inhabitants of the earth—to every nation, tribe, language, and people. 7 He spoke with a loud voice: "Fear God and give Him glory, because the hour of His judgment has come. Worship the Maker of heaven and earth, the sea and springs of water."

Many white supremacists of this century, and slavers from previous centuries, have made claims that "Christ has died for white men only," (Hutton, p. 33) This absurd and abominable claim is here dashed to the garbage it came from by the declaration in Revelation 14 that the good news is for EVERY nation, tribe, language and people.

20. Colossians 3:11-15 11 In Christ there is not Greek and Jew, circumcision and uncircumcision, barbarian, Scythian, slave and free; but Christ is all and in all. 12 Therefore, God's chosen ones, holy and loved, put on heartfelt compassion, kindness, humility, gentleness, and patience, 13 accepting one another and forgiving one another if anyone has a complaint against another. Just as the Lord has forgiven you, so you must also forgive. 14 Above all, put on love—the perfect bond of unity. 15 And let the peace of the Messiah, to which you were also called in one body, control your hearts.

As has already been declared, in Christ all outward distinctions are abolished. The implications of that fact are that Christians must therefore clothe themselves with heartfelt compassion, kindness, humility, gentleness and patience, which leads to accepting and forgiving one another.

6

Does the Bible Condone Slavery?

"And the same law commands "not to muzzle the ox which treadeth out the corn: for the labourer must be reckoned worthy of his food." And it prohibits an ox and ass to be yoked in the plow together pointing perhaps to the want of agreement in the case of the animals; and at the same time teaching not to wrong any one belonging to another race, and bring him under the yoke, when there is no other cause to allege than difference of race, which is no cause at all, being neither wickedness nor the effect of wickedness." Clement of Alexandria, Christian theologian who lived from 150 AD – 215 AD, The Ante-Nicene Fathers (Buffalo, NY: Christian Literature Company, 1885), 368.

"God, who produces and gives breath to men, willed that all should be equal, that is, equally matched. He has imposed the same condition of living on all. He has opened wisdom to all. He has promised immortality to all. No one is cut off from His heavenly benefits.... In His sight, no one is a slave; no one is a master. For if all have the same Father, by an equal right we are all children. No one is poor in the sight of God but he who is without justice. No one is rich, but he who is full of virtues.... For this reason, neither the Romans nor the Greeks could possess justice. For they had men differing from one another by many degrees: the poor and the rich, the humble and the powerful, private persons and the highest authorities of kings. However, where all persons are not equally matched, there is no justice. And, by its nature, inequality excludes

44

justice....

However, someone will say, "Are there not among you some who are poor and others who are rich? Are not some servants and others masters? Is there not some difference between individuals?" There is none. Nor is there any other cause why we mutually bestow upon each other the name of brothers, except that we believe ourselves to be equal. We measure all human things by the spirit, not by the body. Although the condition of our bodies is different, yet we have no servants. For we both regard and speak of them as brothers in spirit and as fellow-servants in religion.... Therefore, in lowliness of mind, we are on an equality: the free with the slaves and the rich with the poor. Nevertheless, in the sight of God we are distinguished only by virtue....

The person who has conducted himself not only as an equal, but even as an inferior, he will plainly obtain a much higher rank of dignity in the judgment of God. Lactantius, circa 305 AD, quoted in: A Dictionary of Early Christian Beliefs: A Reference Guide to More than 700 Topics Discussed by the Early Church Fathers (Peabody, MA: Hendrickson Publishers, 1998), 236.

The above passages, and dozens of others like them, demonstrate the views that the early church had about slavery and race. While there were indeed bond-servants in the early church, both slaves and rich, laborers and merchants, foreigners and natives, were all accorded the title, "brother."

Although the church in latter years would too often give in to opulence and worldliness, the church in the first few centuries carefully sought to heed Paul and James' biblical warnings against showing favoritism and partiality towards anyone. To read Lactantius' words, written around 300 AD, is to read refreshing words of equality and unity, the likes of which the modern world has yet to fully grasp, even 1700 years later.

In October of 2014, Boston Globe columnist and spirituality writer

Margery Eagan related the following experience from her Catholic church, and left dangling a provocative question: Since the Bible condones slavery (and the modern church does not), should not the modern church "discount and dismiss" what Paul said about homosexuality? Here's her column in full:

> At Mass on Wednesday, the reading was St. Paul's letter to the Ephesians, 6:1-9. It reads in part, "Slaves, be obedient to your human masters with fear and trembling." The words are always jarring. In this letter, and others, Paul seems to condone slavery, and biblical scholars have long debated what Paul actually believed about slavery. We do know this: his letters have been quoted throughout history, including in the pre-Civil War United States, to justify it.
>
> The priest at Mass on Wednesday, a wonderful priest, did what many do after this upsetting reading. He explained that Paul's words don't actually mean the Church or Jesus himself condoned slavery. He said that Paul lived in a very "different time," the Roman Empire, 2,000 years ago. Slavery, tragically, was ubiquitous. And Paul was a product of that ancient world with laws and customs today's world would reject.
>
> Hearing all this, again, I was left with my perpetual question. In Romans, Corinthians, and Timothy 1, Paul also condemns homosexuality. And those letters, too, have been quoted through-out Christian history to justify treating gay men and woman differently, even to reject them. So how is it that we don't hear the same "different time" explainers about Paul and gay people? How is it that the Church has found a way to discount and dismiss what Paul said repeatedly about slaves, but not discount and dismiss what he said repeatedly about gays? I don't have the answer. I simply ask the question. (Source: Boston Globe site "Cruxnow.com, October 30, 2014)

The subject of homosexuality will be the focus of an upcoming full-length book in this series (WTBRS - *What the Bible Really Says*), so I won't delve deeply into it here, but I do want to address, and perhaps challenge, the first part of Margery's question, since most people assume it to be true. Does the Bible, the New Testament in particular, actually condone slavery? The answer to that question is, as one would imagine, quite complex. In moving towards an accurate answer, the next chapter will examine 15 key biblical texts on the subject of slavery. Before we go there, however, a brief word on two major ways to interpret the teachings of the Bible will be helpful.

The Bible has been tragically used and abused for centuries in the name of propping up one false ideology or the other. This dynamic happens when humans seek to read INTO the Bible their own beliefs and search out phrases, words and stories to justify themselves, rather than reading OUT of the Bible truths for life.

I teach survey-level New Testament and Old Testament courses at a local liberal arts college. At the beginning of each of those classes, I take a Bible and physically demonstrate two different approaches to Scripture. Holding it over my head, I explain that we can view the Word of God as authoritative - that we must follow it and submit to it - we can't read into the Bible our worldview, biases and feelings, but we must read out of it the foundation for our worldview, biases and feelings. The view that the Bible is above us represents a high view of Scripture - that it is God's Word (not the word of man) and that we must seek to understand what is written and follow it. When we understand the grammar, vocabulary and context of a passage, in other words, we will know the meaning of that passage.

The second major way we can approach Scripture, I demonstrate by putting the Bible on the floor, and explain to the students that in this approach, the Bible is beneath us, and rather than read out of Scripture authoritative direction, we read into Scripture our own views, picking and choosing which Scriptures to follow and which to reject, and interpreting what the Bible has to say in light of our own views and opinions. With this approach, some Bible passages are ignored, or completely reinterpreted by us to mean something entirely different than what the grammar, vocabulary and context of the verse says.

There are technical terms for both of these different approaches to Scripture, with eisegesis denoting the approach that seeks to read meanings _into_ the Bible text, and exegesis indicating the approach that seeks to bring _out of the text_ its intentions and meaning. Dr. James White offers an excellent definition of eisegesis below, and shows how it differs from an exegetical approach:

> _Eisegesis is the reading into a text, in this case, an ancient text of the Bible, of a meaning that is not supported by the grammar, syntax, lexical meanings, and over-all context, of the original. It is the opposite of exegesis, where you read out of the text its original meaning by careful attention to the same things, grammar, syntax, the lexical meanings of the words used by the author (as they were used in his day and in his area), and the over-all context of the document. As common as it is, it should be something the Christian minister finds abhorrent, for when you stop and think about it, eisegesis muffles the voice of God. If the text of Scripture is in fact God-breathed (2 Tim. 3:16) and if God speaks in the entirety of the Bible (Matt. 22:31) then eisegesis would involve silencing that divine voice and replacing it with the thoughts, intents, and most often, traditions, of the one doing the interpretation. In fact, in my experience, eisegetical mishandling of the inspired text is the single most common source of heresy, division, disunity, and a lack of clarity in the proclamation of the gospel._ (Dr. James White – Pulpit Crimes, 2006)

Almost all Christians have engaged in eisegesis at some point, but it is a very dangerous practice. Unfortunately, my use of the word "dangerous" here is quite literal. Eisegetical methods of interpretation have led to much bloodshed and acrimony between people who call themselves Christians. There have been wars and killings and thousands of denominational splits, all because we humans have a tendency to look to Scripture for divine approval of our thoughts, actions and opinions, rather than seeking to base our thoughts, actions and opinions on a right understanding of Scripture.

Supporters of race-based slavery have engaged in significant and aberrant eisegesis in reading into Scripture Divine commendation for their abominable practices. While it is true that the Bible does not completely ban the practice of bond-servitude, a careful examination of Scripture will demonstrate that the bond-servitude of the Bible and the race-based slavery of Europe and the Americas are vastly different.

I'd like to share a very interesting, and extremely important piece of history as a way to close out this chapter, and bridge into the discussion of the next chapter. The passage below is one of the earliest descriptions of Jesus and His followers by somebody not in the Bible. It was written by the Roman governor of Bithynia, a man named Pliny the younger, and was addressed to the Roman emperor Trajan. The date of writing was approximately 112 AD, and Pliny is writing to inform the emperor of a new movement of people who worship Christ as a God, and bind themselves to pledges to not steal, commit adultery, lie, or be untrustworthy. Pliny was very concerned about these strange people, because they appeared to him to be members of a secret society, which he had forbidden in his district. Therefore, he captured two young girls and interrogated them to find out the truth about these Jesus-followers. Note below how the two young girls are ministers (deaconesses) in the church AND they are slaves/bond-servants. This is steady proof, from an outside source, that the early church viewed slaves as worthy and qualified for some of the most crucial positions that the church had to offer!

They declared that all the wrong they had committed, wittingly or unwittingly, was this, that they had been accustomed on a fixed day to meet before dawn and sing antiphonally a hymn to Christ as a god, and bind themselves by a solemn pledge (sacramento) not to commit any enormity, but to abstain from theft, brigandage, and adultery, to keep their word, and not to refuse to restore what had been entrusted to their charge if demanded. After these ceremonies they used to disperse and assemble again to share a common meal of innocent food, and even this they had given up after I had issued the edict by which, according to your instructions, I prohibited secret societies (hetaeriae).

I therefore considered it the more necessary, in order to ascertain what truth there was in this account, to examine two slave-girls, who were called deaconesses (ministrae), *and even to use torture. I found nothing except a perverted and unbounded superstition. I therefore have adjourned the investigation and hastened to consult you, for I thought the matter was worth consulting you about, especially on account of the numbers who are involved. For many of every age and rank, and of both sexes, are already and will be summoned to stand their trial. For this superstition has infected not only the towns, but also the villages and country; yet it apparently can be checked and corrected. (Source: F. H. Blackburne Daniell, "Trajanus (1), M. Ulpius (Nerva)," ed. William Smith and Henry Wace, A Dictionary of Christian Biography, Literature, Sects and Doctrines (London: John Murray, 1877–1887), 1040.)*

7

15 Foundational Bible Passages on Slavery

More than that, the gospel has a consuming power... Once fairly set alight, it will burn, and blaze, and spread till others shall cast away their evil habits, and turn unto the living God. I cannot help noticing in history the consuming power of the gospel of Christ.

There have been old systems of iniquity that have been hoary with age, but when, at last, they have been attacked by the Church of God with the sword of the Spirit, and the gospel of Christ, they have been utterly destroyed. **There was, for instance, that abominable institution of slavery, and there was a part of the Church of Christ which tried to palliate it, and spoke of it as "a divine institution, a peculiar institution," and I know not what; but when the Church of God denounced slavery as a thing utterly inconsistent with Christianity, the thing was burnt up right speedily, and passed away.**

There are many more social and political wrongs that will have to perish through the burning power of the gospel; and there is much in our hearts, and much in our lives, and much all round about us that will have to go as the gospel fire burns more and more vigorously. But remember that it must be God's Word that will burn out the evil. We cannot do much with our poor thinkings and tinkerings; it is the eternal truth, the everlasting verities, brought to bear upon the sons of men, that shall soon separate between the dross and the gold, consuming the one and leaving the other pure. (Source: C. H. Spurgeon, "God's Fire and Hammer," in The Metropolitan Tabernacle Pulpit Sermons, vol. 42 (London: Passmore & Alabaster, 1896), 172. Note: This message was preached by Spurgeon in 1886)

Do you not mark how God hath followed you with plagues, and may not conscience tell you, that it is for your inhumanity to the souls and bodies of men – **To go as pirates and catch up poor Negroes, or people of another land that never forfeited life or liberty, and to make them slaves, and fell them, is one of the worst kind of thievery in the world,** *and such persons are to be taken for the* *common enemies of mankind; and they that buy them as beasts, for their mere commodity, and betray or destroy or neglect their souls, are **fitter to be called devils than Christians**. It is an heinous sin to buy them...because by right the man is his own; therefore no man else can have a just title to him. Richard Baxter, a Puritan preacher and writer from the 1600s. (Source: The Practical Works of Richard Baxter)*

Consider with yourselves, if you were in the same condition as the blacks are, who came strangers to you, and were sold to you as slaves. I say, if this should be the condition of your or yours, you would think it hard to measure. Yea, and a very great bondage and cruelty. And therefore, consider seriously of this, and do you for and to them, or any other, to do unto you, were you in like slavish condition; and bring them to know the Lord Christ. George Fox, Quaker preacher, 1671. (Source: Source: A caution and warning to Great-Britain and her colonies, in a Short representation of the calamitous state of the Enslaved Negroes in the British Dominions : Collected from various Authors, and submitted to the Serious consideration of all, more especially of those in power. By Anthony Benezet and William Warburton, 1779.)

We ourselves, who profess to be Christians, and boast of the peculiar advantage we enjoy, by means of express revelation of our duty from heaven, are in effect just like these very untaught and rude heathen countries. With all our superior light, we instill into those, whom we call savage and barbarous, the most despicable opinion of human nature. We, to the utmost of our power, weaken and dissolve the universal tie that binds and unites mankind. We practice what we would exclaim against, as the utmost excess of cruelty and tyranny, if nations of the world, differing in colour, were possessed of empire, as to be able to reduce us to a state of unmerited and brutish servitude. Of consequence, we sacrifice our reason, our humanity, our Christianity, to an unnatural sordid gain. We teach other nations to despise and trample under foot all obligations of social virtue. We take the most effectual method to prevent the propagation of the gospel by representing it as a scheme of power and barbarous oppression, and an enemy to the natural privileges and rights of men.

Perhaps all that I have now offered may be of very little weight to restrain this enormity, this aggravated iniquity. However, I shall still have the satisfaction of having entered my private protest against a practice which, in my opinion, buds that God, who is the God and Father of the Gentiles, unconverted to Christianity, most daring and bold defiance, and spurns at all the principles, both of natural and revealed religion. James Foster. (Source: Discourses on All the Principle Branches of Natural Religion and Social Virture, 1749)

The issue of racism and the Bible, as we have seen, is actually a fairly simple one. The Bible heartily and wholly condemns racism of any kind, and unequivocally declares that all humans are equally made in the Image of God, and equally related to each other through Adam and Eve. God shows no partiality, and the gospel and its benefits are for every tribe, nation, tongue and people.

Less simple is the topic of slavery and the Bible, primarily because the writers of the Bible acknowledge the existence of slavery but are not wholly concerned with toppling the institution. Before we discuss the particulars of why that might be, it is important to consider an overview of what exactly the Bible does teach about slavery.

The majority of the passages below will be New Testament passages. This does not discount the teaching of the Old Testament, but it is a recognition that Christians of the past 19 centuries have been *primarily* governed by the New Testament. The Old Testament was written to the Jewish people, and it is Scripture and profitable for Christians today, but the New Testament is binding and authoritative for Christians today, an issue that was settled during the church's first council, as recorded in Acts 15:

Therefore, in my judgment, we should not cause difficulties for those among the Gentiles who turn to God, 20 but instead we should write to them to abstain from things polluted by idols, from sexual immorality, from eating anything that has been strangled, and from blood. 21 For since ancient times, Moses has had those who proclaim him in every city, and every Sabbath day he is read aloud in the synagogues." 22 Then the apostles and the elders, with the whole church, decided to select men who were among them and to send them to Antioch with Paul and Barnabas: Judas, called Barsabbas, and Silas, both leading men among the brothers. 23 They wrote this letter to be delivered by them:

From the apostles and the elders, your brothers,

To the brothers among the Gentiles in Antioch, Syria, and Cilicia: Greetings. 24 Because we have heard that some without our authorization went out from us and troubled you with their words and unsettled your hearts, 25 we have unanimously decided to select men and send them to you along with our dearly loved Barnabas and Paul, 26 who have risked their lives for the name of our Lord Jesus Christ. 27 Therefore we have sent Judas and Silas, who will personally report the same things by word of mouth. 28 For it was the Holy Spirit's decision—and ours—to put no greater burden on you than these necessary things: 29 that you abstain from food offered to idols, from blood, from eating anything that has been strangled, and from sexual immorality. You will do well if you keep yourselves from these things. (Acts 15:20-29)

I believe that passages like Acts 15, above, Romans 7:6 ("*But now we have been released from the law, since we have died to what held us, so that we may serve in the new way of the Spirit and not in the old letter of the law*"), and Ephesians 2:15 ("*He made of no effect the law consisting of commands and expressed in regulations, so that He might create in Himself one new man from the two, resulting in peace*"), indicate that Christians are no longer under the authority of the Old Testament, but under the authority of the New Testament. (Please read below, at the end of the chapter, for Dr. Douglas Moo's far more thorough treatment of this subject.)

Therefore, when it comes to the issue of slavery, Christians do not appeal first to the Old Testament for answers and guidance, but the New, a reality that is reflected below. Unless otherwise noted, each passage is from the English Standard Version (ESV.)

1. *Philemon: Paul, a prisoner of Christ Jesus, and Timothy our brother:*
To Philemon our dear friend and coworker, 2 to Apphia our sister, to Archippus our fellow soldier, and to the church that meets in your home...
8 For this reason, although I have great boldness in Christ to command you to do what is right, 9 I appeal to you, instead, on the basis of love. I, Paul, as an elderly man and now also as a prisoner of Christ Jesus, 10 appeal to you for my son, Onesimus. I fathered him while I was in chains. 11 Once he was useless to you, but now he is useful both to you and to me. 12 I am sending him back to you as a part of myself. 13 I wanted to keep him with me, so that in my imprisonment for the gospel he might serve me in your place. 14 But I didn't want to do anything without your consent, so that your good deed might not be out of obligation, but of your own free will. 15 For perhaps this is why he was separated from you for a brief time, so that you might get him back permanently, 16 no longer as a slave, but more than a

slave—as a dearly loved brother. He is especially so to me, but even more to you, both in the flesh and in the Lord.

17 So if you consider me a partner, accept him as you would me. 18 And if he has wronged you in any way, or owes you anything, charge that to my account. 19 I, Paul, write this with my own hand: I will repay it—not to mention to you that you owe me even your own self. 20 Yes, brother, may I have joy from you in the Lord; refresh my heart in Christ. 21 Since I am confident of your obedience, I am writing to you, knowing that you will do even more than I say. 22 But meanwhile, also prepare a guest room for me, for I hope that through your prayers I will be restored to you.

Yes – there is an entire book of the New Testament, Paul's letter to Philemon, that is concerned with the issue of slavery. Philemon is a Christian and a slave owner (!) that is a friend of Paul, and was apparently saved through Paul's ministry. Paul doesn't *directly* ask Philemon to release Onesimus, but you could argue that he absolutely does ask for, and even command, the release of Onesimus, a fact made obvious by vs. 14 ("your good deed."), vs. 16 (no longer a slave!), vs. 19 (Paul will repay any debt of Onesimus) and vs. 21 ("Since I am confident of your **obedience. I know you will do more than I say**")

Even if one doesn't fully agree with that premise, it is unquestionable that Paul directs Philemon to no longer consider Onesimus a slave, but to treat him as Philemon would treat Paul – a lofty command, to be sure. While the Bible doesn't indicate whether Philemon followed Paul's directive or not, church history tells us that he did, and Onesimus went on to become a bishop in the early church. Henry Halley tells the story in his Bible handbook:

The Bible gives no hint as to how the master received his returning slave. But there is a tradition that says his master did receive him, and took Paul's veiled hint and gave the slave his liberty. That is the way the Gospel works. Christ in the heart of the slave made the slave recognize the social usages of his day, and go back to his master determined to be a good slave and live out his natural life as a slave. Christ in the heart of the master made the master recognize the slave as a Christian brother and give him his liberty. There is a tradition that Onesimus afterward became a bishop of Berea.

The Mosaic slave laws and the writings of Paul benefited and protected the slaves as best as possible in their situation. God's desire for any who are enslaved is freedom (Luke 4:18; Gal. 5:1). Those who are set free in Christ then need to be prepared to walk in liberty. Pagan nations had a much different outlook toward slaves, believing slaves had no rights or privileges. Because of the restrictions and humane aspect of the Mosaic laws on slavery, it never existed on a large scale in Israel, and did not exhibit the cruelties seen in Egypt, Greece, Rome, Assyria and other nations. (Source: Henry Halley's Bible Handbook with the New International Version, 2008)

2. *Exodus 13:3 and 13:14-15* 3 **Then Moses said to the people, "Remember this day when you came out of Egypt, out of the place of slavery, for the Lord brought you out of here by the strength of His hand. vss. 14 "In the future, when your son asks you, 'What does this mean?' say to him, 'By the strength of His hand the Lord brought us out of Egypt, out of the place of slavery.**

It should be remembered, that the Israelites themselves started out as slaves, aliens and strangers in a strange land. They were under the yolk of slavery for over 400 years, a fact prophesied by God to Abraham in Genesis 15. The Israelites knew first hand the horrors of slavery for centuries.

3. *Matthew 6:24* **"No one can be a slave of two masters, since either he will hate one and love the other, or be devoted to one**

and despise the other. You cannot be slaves of God and of money.

This is Jesus' first mention of slavery, and it is interesting on two different counts. First, Jesus demonstrates here that one can be a slave and love one's master. Second, it introduces us to the New Testament use of the word "slave." In this particular instance, the word Jesus uses is the verb "*douleuō*" which means either to be a slave OR to be a servant. The same verb is used in Luke 15:29, "*but he answered his father, 'Look, these many years I have served you, and I never disobeyed your command, yet you never gave me a young goat, that I might celebrate with my friends.*"

In this case, the verb is used by the elder brother in Jesus' famous parable of the prodigal son. The elder brother was obviously not a slave in his father's household, but he did work and serve his father. The fact is that the Greek verb "*douleuō*" and the Greek noun "*doulos*" from which it is derived can be used to indicate either slavery or service, and the meaning of the word is probably more in line with our English word servant, than our connotations of the word "slave." As we will look at in a couple of chapters, the English word "slave." and the New Testament word "*doulos*" are not very similar.

> 4. *Matthew 20:26-28* **It shall not be so among you. But whoever would be great among you must be your servant, 27 and whoever would be first among you must be your slave, 28 even as the Son of Man came not to be served but to serve, and to give his life as a ransom for many."**

In vs 26, the word used by Jesus that the ESV translates as "servant," is the Greek word "*diakonos*" and the word that Jesus uses in vs 27, translated as "slave," is "*doulos*" *Diakono*s is the Greek word that was used for somebody who waited on tables in the first century – a server. It was co-opted by the church to mean "deacon," in Acts 6, and ultimately came to also mean "minister." Jesus' teaching here is revolutionary – He is saying that the key to greatness, and the key to becoming first, or chief, is to be a servant or slave. In context, it appears that the words servant and slave are used very similarly here by Jesus, and they are used *glowingly*. In the upside-down kingdom of Jesus, being a servant is being great, and being a slave is opening the door to being chief. This proclamation goes right along with Jesus' teaching in Mark 10:31, "*Many who are first will be last,*" in the Kingdom of Heaven and eternity.

5. Romans 6: 15-23 15 **What then? Are we to sin because we are not under law but under grace? By no means! 16 Do you not know that if you present yourselves to anyone as obedient slaves, you are slaves of the one whom you obey, either of sin, which leads to death, or of obedience, which leads to righteousness? 17 But thanks be to God, that you who were once slaves of sin have become obedient from the heart to the standard of teaching to which you were committed, 18 and, having been set free from sin, have become slaves of righteousness. 19 I am speaking in human terms, because of your natural limitations. For just as you once presented your members as slaves to impurity and to lawlessness leading to more lawlessness, so now present your members as slaves to righteousness leading to sanctification. 20 For when you were slaves of sin, you were free in regard to righteousness. 21 But what fruit were you getting at that time from the things of which you are now ashamed? For the end of those things is death. 22 But now that you have been set free from sin and have become slaves of God, the fruit you get leads to sanctification and its end, eternal life. 23 For the wages of sin is death, but the free gift of God is eternal life in Christ Jesus our Lord.**

The word "bond-servant" (*doulos*) appears in about 36 verses in the New Testament, with Romans 6 and Galatians 4 being the two densest discussions of the topic. While Paul's discussion of slavery (or bond-servitude) here is largely metaphoric, there are still two noteworthy facts about slavery in the Bible found in this passage. First, as indicated by vs. 16, New Testament slavery does carry implications of obedience. Second, Paul here contrasts two polar opposites that humans will serve: Either they will be slaves to sin, a terrible master that brings only death, or they will be slaves to God, a master that brings freedom, sanctification, and eternal life.

In Pauline theology, all humans are slaves to something, a fact that has extreme implications when discussing the complicated issue of slavery in the Bible. In the way that Paul discusses slavery, the key question relates to how good the master is. If the master is sin itself, or a cruel human, then slavery is a terrible evil. If the master is God, or a Godly human, then servant-hood is very different.

American Christians, no matter their race, hopefully cringe in their inner selves when they hear the word slavery. The system of slavery in America from its inception until the late 19th century was race-based, cruel, godless, and diametrically opposed to the understanding of slavery in the Bible. Slavery in the Bible was far more similar to what we think of when we think of somebody serving as a butler, or a housekeeper, or a groundskeeper. No, it wasn't a glorious position, and yes, sometimes slaves were taken advantage of, but first century slavery, at least the type discussed in the New Testament, was NOT race-based, and shared little in common with the race-based slavery of England and the Americas. Much more on that in chapter 9.

The idea of being slaves to God or Christ is a recurring theme in the New Testament, far more prevalent than is commonly understood, appearing in **Matthew 6:24, Matthew 22:3-10, Mark 13:34, Luke 12:37, Luke 12:38, Luke 12:45, Luke 17:10!, John 15:15, Acts 2:18, Acts 4:29, Acts 16:17, Ephesians 6:6, Philippians 1:1, Colossians 3:24, 1 Peter 2:16, Romans 6:22, Romans 16:18, Revelation 1:1, Revelation 2:20, Revelation 6:11, Revelation 7:3, Revelation 19:2, Revelation 19:5, Revelation 22:3, and Revelation 22:6, and quite possibly at least a dozen other verses.** The most frequent name used to designate general followers of Jesus in the New Testament is the word "brothers." Unless I am mistaken, the second most frequent name for general followers of Jesus in the New Testament is "slave/servant/*doulos*." (The word "disciple"also frequently refers to followers of Jesus, but is more often applied to the original 12 disciples of Jesus, and is not used at all after the book of Acts)

Let this idea sink in, because it is crucial: followers of God, according to the Bible, are slaves/servants/*douloses* of Him. To be a servant is not a bad thing, according to Jesus, but is the very key to greatness. Americans and Westerners look down on serving and servitude, but Jesus practically glorified it. That acknowledged, I want to reiterate that race-based slavery is a cruel and horrid abomination, and its perpetrators deserve nothing more than derision.

> *6. Luke 17:7-10 "Will any one of you who has a servant plowing or keeping sheep say to him when he has come in from the field, 'Come at once and recline at table'? 8 Will he not rather say to him, 'Prepare supper for me, and dress properly, and serve me while I eat and drink, and afterward you will eat and drink'? 9 Does he thank the servant because he did what was commanded? 10 So you also, when you have done all that you were commanded, say, 'We are unworthy servants; we have only done what was our duty.'"*

This passage will likely come as a shock to many who read it. Jesus here addresses those who had slaves, and He did not immediately tell them to release their slaves! That is astonishing to us, until we remember that slavery during Jesus time was fundamentally different than race-based slavery in the Americas and United Kingdom. We learn two things about slavery during biblical times here. First, that servants/slaves are expected to obey their masters and tend to their needs. Second, that followers of Jesus should not expect commendation, but should obey with extreme humility.

7. Luke 12:35-40 "Stay dressed for action and keep your lamps burning, 36 and be like men who are waiting for their master to come home from the wedding feast, so that they may open the door to him at once when he comes and knocks. 37 Blessed are those servants whom the master finds awake when he comes. Truly, I say to you, he will dress himself for service and have them recline at table, and he will come and serve them. 38 If he comes in the second watch, or in the third, and finds them awake, blessed are those servants! 39 But know this, that if the master of the house had known at what hour the thief was coming, he would not have left his house to be broken into. 40 You also must be ready, for the Son of Man is coming at an hour you do not expect."

As shocking as passage number six is, I would argue that passage #7 is even more shocking. In this teaching of Jesus, He notes that those slaves/servants who are watchfully waiting for their master's return (The second coming of Jesus) will be rewarded by getting to sit down at the master's table and actually enjoy being served by the master himself. What an incredible idea – that the master, Jesus, will serve His faithful servants at His table when He returns.

8. 1 Corinthians 12:12-14 12 For just as the body is one and has many members, and all the members of the body, though many, are one body, so it is with Christ. 13 For in one Spirit we were all baptized into one body—Jews or Greeks, slaves or free—and all were made to drink of one Spirit.

The early church was made up of slaves, freeman and nobles. It was composed of Jews, Greeks, Romans and other 'barbarians.' There were all shades of skin color, and all manner of economic class together when the early church met. Sometimes, this dynamic led to favoritism and partiality, but multiple times in Scripture, the church was sternly warned to not give any place to favoring one people group over another. As Paul notes here in 1 Corinthians 12, all of the members - slave or free - were baptized by ONE Spirit into ONE Body. The coming of Christ Jesus, His death on the cross and His resurrection has destroyed every dividing wall in humanity, a truth powerfully proclaimed by Paul in Ephesians 2: 13-19:

> *But now in Christ Jesus you who once were far off have been brought near by the blood of Christ. 14 For he himself is our peace, who has made us both one and has broken down in his flesh the dividing wall of hostility 15 by abolishing the law of commandments expressed in ordinances, that he might create in himself one new man in place of the two, so making peace, 16 and might reconcile us both to God in one body through the cross, thereby killing the hostility. 17 And he came and preached peace to you who were far off and peace to those who were near. 18 For through him we both have access in one Spirit to the Father. 19 So then you are no longer strangers and aliens, but you are fellow citizens with the saints and members of the household of God,*

To reiterate: Slaves, free, nobles, rich, poor, Gentiles, Jews, strangers, aliens and the like are all now saints, citizens, members of the household of God, and co-heirs with Christ. All other titles and positions are meaningless.

> 9. *2 Corinthians 4:5 For we are not proclaiming ourselves but Jesus Christ as Lord, and ourselves as your slaves because of Jesus.*

Once again we see a normative New Testament usage of the word *doulos*/servant/slave. Paul is proclaiming that he and his apostle team are 'slaves' to the Corinthians. In doing so, he is also demonstrating the lack of racial baggage that adhered to the word *doulos* in the first century.

> 10 *Galatians 4:1-7 I mean that the heir, as long as he is a child, is no different from a slave, though he is the owner of everything, 2 but he is under guardians and managers until the date set by his father. 3 In the same way we also, when we were children, were enslaved to the elementary principles of the world. 4 But when the fullness of time had come, God sent forth his Son, born of woman, born under the law, 5 to redeem those who were under the law, so that we might receive adoption as sons. 6 And because you are sons, God has sent the Spirit of his Son into our hearts, crying, "Abba! Father!" 7 So you are no longer a slave, but a son, and if a son, then an heir through God.*

That Paul uses the term "doulos/servant/slave" to refer to a child in his father's household here demonstrates with extreme clarity that the New Testament use of the word 'slave' or bond-servant is far different from the race-based slavery of the Americas and the United Kingdom. No American slaveholder in the 1800s would have referred to his young son as a slave, but Paul uses precisely this illustrative word to describe a son that was not yet old enough to inherit his father's finances and estates. The difference between this concept and race-based slavery could not be more pronounced.

Also of note here is Paul's teaching that those who have been saved by Jesus and indwelt by His Holy Spirit are no longer slaves, but are now sons of God AND heirs of God. Jesus uses similar language in John 15:15, when He says, *"I no longer call you slaves/servants/doulos, for the slave/servant/doulos does not know what his master is doing; but I have called you friends, for all that I have heard from my Father I have made known to you."*

Keep in mind, however, that Jesus disciples continued to identify themselves as slaves/servants/*douloses* of Christ after John 15:15, and Paul continued to call himself the same, even after he wrote about the wonderful truths of sonship in Galatians 4. For a Christian, there will always be a tension between our servanthood and our sonship.

> 11. *Galatians 11:21-31 Tell me, you who desire to be under the law, do you not listen to the law? 22 For it is written that Abraham had two sons, one by a slave woman and one by a free woman. 23 But the son of the slave was born according to the flesh, while the son of the free woman was born through promise. 24 Now this may be interpreted allegorically: these women are two covenants. One is from Mount Sinai, bearing children for slavery; she is Hagar. 25 Now Hagar is Mount Sinai in Arabia; she corresponds to the present Jerusalem, for she is in slavery with her children. 26 But the Jerusalem above is free, and she is our mother. 27 For it is written, "Rejoice, O barren one who does not bear; break forth and cry aloud, you who are not in labor! For the children of the desolate one will be more than those of the one who has a husband." 28 Now you, brothers, like Isaac, are children of promise. 29 But just as at that time he who was born according to the flesh persecuted him who was born according to the Spirit, so also it is now. 30 But what does the Scripture say? "Cast out the slave woman and her son, for the son of the slave woman shall not inherit with the son of the free woman." 31 So, brothers, we are not children of the slave but of the free woman.*

Paul was fully aware, in composing the above contrast between being children of a slave woman and children of a free woman, that many of his hearers and readers would themselves be *doulois*/servants/slaves. His message to his hearers who were in that position was simple: They might be *doulois*/servants/slaves in the natural world, but in Christ, and therefore, in eternity, they were NOT the sons of slavery, but instead the sons of freedom.

> 12. *Hebrews 2:14-17 Since therefore the children share in flesh*

and blood, he himself likewise partook of the same things, that through death he might destroy the one who has the power of death, that is, the devil, 15 and deliver all those who through fear of death were subject to lifelong slavery. 16 For surely it is not angels that he helps, but he helps the offspring of Abraham. 17 Therefore he had to be made like his brothers in every respect, so that he might become a merciful and faithful high priest in the service of God, to make propitiation for the sins of the people.

Hebrews 2 has little to say in regards to the practical issue of slavery, but the theological truths in it are so rich that they must be covered here. According to the Bible, the worst kind of slavery is not the kind that involves being enslaved to a cruel and wicked master. As bad as that is, it is far worse to be enslaved to death and Satan. Hebrews 2 here demonstrates the wonderful news that Jesus, through His own righteous death, permanently broke the bonds of death and Hell that had previously held all humanity in captivity as slaves. Jesus is the first and ultimate abolitionist.

13. Ephesians 6:5-9 Bondservants, obey your earthly masters with fear and trembling, with a sincere heart, as you would Christ, 6 not by the way of eye-service, as people-pleasers, but as bondservants of Christ, doing the will of God from the heart, 7 rendering service with a good will as to the Lord and not to man, 8 knowing that whatever good anyone does, this he will receive back from the Lord, whether he is a bondservant or is free. 9 Masters, do the same to them, and stop your threatening, knowing that he who is both their Master and yours is in heaven, and that there is no partiality with him.

The translators of the English Standard Version of the Bible here opted to use "bond-servants" instead of slaves. It is a translation call that I absolutely agree with, but it should be noted that the word in question is the same "*doulos*/servant/slave." word we have been discussing at length in this chapter.

Here are commands given by Paul as to how bond-servants or slaves are to behave. They are to obey and follow the directions of their earthly masters with respect, and they are to work hard, as if they were working hard for God. The good news is that God Himself will ultimately reward them for their good and conscientious service. Masters, similarly, are to treat their servants well and are never allowed to threaten them. Masters are to keep in mind that they are equal with their slaves in the eyes of God, who shows no favoritism or partiality towards rich or poor.

This is another challenging passage, and it has at least three other parallels in 1 Timothy 6:1 and Titus 2:9 and 1 Peter 2:18. The Bible simply does not view submission to other people nearly as negatively as we do in the 21st century; in fact, the Bible honors and upholds the ideals of submission as a good and honorable practice. To be sure, I need to take the opportunity to remind us once again that the kind of slavery/servanthood spoken of in the New Testament is NOT at all of the same tenor as the type of race-based slavery that moderns are more familiar with. Paul is here telling bond-servants, to obey their bosses, because 1st century bond-servitude was vastly different from the disgusting system of chattal slavery in the Americas.

> *14. Titus 2:9 Bondservants are to be submissive to their own masters in everything; they are to be well-pleasing, not argumentative, 10 not pilfering, but showing all good faith, so that in everything they may adorn the doctrine of God our Savior.*

Paul! Why in the world are you telling bond-servants to actually be submissive to their masters? How can you command that they be well-pleasing, display good faith, and not be argumentative?? I obviously cannot speak for Paul, but the answer must be something along the lines of this: Submission by somebody who is mindful of

God demonstrates such a beautiful testimony that it literally adorns and decorates the doctrine of God. In other words, the submission of a Godly servant makes the truths of the Bible somehow more beautiful.

15. 1 Peter 2: 9 But you are a chosen race, a royal priesthood, a holy nation, a people for his own possession, that you may proclaim the excellencies of him who called you out of darkness into his marvelous light. 10 Once you were not a people, but now you are God's people; once you had not received mercy, but now you have received mercy...13 Be subject for the Lord's sake to every human institution, whether it be to the emperor as supreme, 14 or to governors as sent by him to punish those who do evil and to praise those who do good. 15 For this is the will of God, that by doing good you should put to silence the ignorance of foolish people. 16 Live as people who are free, not using your freedom as a cover-up for evil, but living as servants of God. 17 Honor everyone. Love the brotherhood. Fear God. Honor the emperor.
18 Servants, be subject to your masters with all respect, not only to the good and gentle but also to the unjust. 19 For this is a gracious thing, when, mindful of God, one endures sorrows while suffering unjustly. 20 For what credit is it if, when you sin and are beaten for it, you endure? But if when you do good and suffer for it you endure, this is a gracious thing in the sight of God. 21 For to this you have been called, because Christ also suffered for you, leaving you an example, so that you might follow in his steps. 22 He committed no sin, neither was deceit found in his mouth. 23 When he was reviled, he did not revile in return; when he suffered, he did not threaten, but continued entrusting himself to him who judges justly. 24 He himself bore our sins in his body on the tree, that we might die to sin and live to righteousness. By his wounds you have been healed. 25 For you were straying like sheep, but have now returned to the Shepherd and Overseer of your souls.

1 Peter 2 is an amazing passage of Scripture that is absolutely stuffed with glorious scriptural truths, beginning with the wonderfully good news that all followers of Jesus are ONE race, ONE priesthood, ONE nation, and ONE people. It also has several stunning and difficult calls to submission. Vs. 13, Peter challengingly calls believers to submit to EVERY human institution, including Godless pagan emperors. Why? Why should we submit to presidents or emperors or rules and regulations that we don't agree with, Peter? Because, Peter notes, when Christians submit in a good and honorable way, they do well, and silence the ignorant complaining of foolish people.

Not only that, but Peter also calls bond-servants to submit to their masters – even to unjust and cruel masters! What a preposterous idea, and yet, in doing so, Christians who suffer well under injustice are following in the footsteps of their master Jesus.

So, what is the conclusion of this complicated question, does the Bible indeed condone slavery? The answers is, yes and no. The first and primary answer is no – the Bible soundly and roundly condemns any sort of race-based slavery, and any sort of slavery that includes kidnapping, violence, coercion, or threatening behavior. On the other hand, the answer is yes: the Bible does condone doulos/servant/slavery, at least in a sense of the word 'condone,' by not calling for the utter abolishment of slavery.

That answer at first might seem wishy-washy, but it accurately reflects the tenor and tone of the Bible's teaching about slavery and servitude. As we have seen above, and will see more in an upcoming chapter, the writers of the Bible, under the inspiration of the Holy Spirit, had no trouble whatsoever referring to themselves as slaves of Christ, and didn't blink an eye about calling followers of Jesus to slavery/servitude of God. The word 'doulos/servant/slave,' though it was a lowly word and position, simply did not carry the same racial baggage and negative connotations to them that it does to us. Writer John Ellis gets it correct in this nuanced discussion of slavery and the

Bible:

It's true that the Bible never explicitly condemns slavery, but it never condones it either. It does regulate, liberally regulates, an already existing institution – an institution that had little resemblance to the slavery found in the American South, by the way.

Right off the bat, Exodus 21:16 flatly forbids and condemns what most people mean when they reference slavery. Look, if God's Word clearly states, and it does, "Whoever steals a man and sells him, and anyone found in possession of him, shall be put to death", it's hard, at least with a straight face, to claim that the Bible condones slavery as defined by 18th and 19th century America. Truth be told, the slavery that the Bible regulates, again, liberally regulates, would be more appropriately termed "indentured servitude." For one thing, there was no racial element involved. For another, slaves were generally prisoners of war or were being punished for a crime – usually a crime involving the failure to pay a debt...

Fair enough, but the Bible is one thing and the Church another, right? I mean, the Church supported slavery, didn't it? Well, no. In fact, many of the Christians and churches that opposed American chattel slavery on moral and religious grounds often pointed to the reality that the version of slavery practiced during Biblical times would not allow for American chattel slavery. Referring to slavery in the Old Testament, Kentucky Baptist preacher James M. Pendleton wrote in the 1840s, "there are points of material dissimilarity between that system and our system of slavery."

One of those "points of material dissimilarity" was that if the Southern slaveholders were to practice the type of slavery that was regulated by the Bible, they would have to enslave whites as well as Africans. Noted historian Mark Noll points to the anti-slavery arguments of Minister John Fee, among others of the time, that the concept of slavery based on race was not only absurd but unbiblical. Unfortunately, this argument failed to make inroads with the Southern slaveholders, and Mark Noll concludes with the telling statement that this failure "reveals that factors other than simple fidelity to Scripture were exerting great influence [over Southern slave-holders]." (Source: https://adayinhiscourt.com)

Douglas Moo on Christians and The Old Testament.

The below is from the Romans volume of the New International Version Application Commentary. In this passage, Dr. Moo is discussing Romans 7, and presenting his viewpoint that Christians are not bound by the laws of the Old Testament (which are still Scripture), but are under the New Testament:

What role does the Old Testament law have in this "law of Christ" that governs Christians? Perhaps the most popular answer among evangelical Christians stems from the Puritan tradition. Puritan theologians made a basic distinction between two different functions of the Mosaic law. On the one hand, it was a "covenant of works" that God established between himself and Israel. God gave Israel his law and demanded that they obey it; if they did not, they would die. On the other hand, the law functioned as a revelation of God's moral will.

Applying this distinction to Paul, the Puritans concluded that when Paul said that believers are no longer "under the law" or that we are released from it, he means that we are no longer under the law as a covenant of works. That is, the law no longer has power to condemn us for our sins. But we are still under the law as a revelation of God's moral will. To be sure, we need no longer obey the civil and ceremonial law, for those parts of the law have been fulfilled in Christ. But an important, indeed a basic, component of the "law of Christ" is the moral law of the Old Testament, manifested especially in the Ten Commandments.

A large swath of contemporary evangelicalism is the heir to this Puritan tradition. We may not use the same terminology they did, but the view of the Mosaic law is similar. This position, however, rests on two distinctions that are not as clear in Paul as we may think they are. The first is the distinction between the law as revelation of God's will and law as covenant of works, or, to phrase it another way, between the commanding function of the law and the condemning function of the law. Paul does not clearly distinguish these. In fact, in texts like 1 Corinthians 9:19–21, it is clear that not being "under the Mosaic law" means "not being under its commands," for the issue there has to do with the way Paul behaves. In other words, it is hard to maintain that being "under the law" in Romans 6:14–15 and being "released from the law" in 7:6 do not include the commanding element of the law.

Equally questionable is the time-honored distinction among the civil, ceremonial, and moral law. Some interpreters use these distinctions to argue, for instance, that Paul is claiming in 6:14–15 and 7:4, 6 only that believers are no longer obliged to obey the civil and/or ceremonial parts of the law. But Jews certainly did not divide up the law in this way, and evidence from the New Testament that early Christians did is slim.

We conclude, then, that we cannot restrict Paul's claim that believers have been "released from the law" to a certain function of the law or to certain parts of the law. The believer has been set free from the commanding authority of the Mosaic law—period. What this means in practice is that no part of the Old Testament law stands any longer as a direct and unmediated guide to Christian living. Like a person who is free from the laws of the state of Indiana because she has moved to Illinois, so Christians are free from the law of the old covenant because we now belong to the new covenant.

Does our freedom from the Old Testament law include even the Ten Commandments? Yes and no. Yes in the sense that those commandments as part of the Mosaic law no longer stand over us. But no in the sense that the teaching of nine of the ten commandments is explicitly taken up by New Testament authors and made part of the "law of Christ."

What all this means in practice, then, is that we should look to the New Testament for those commandments that express God's moral will for us as new covenant Christians. Its teachings, properly interpreted, are to be obeyed. But this does not mean that we should no longer read the Old Testament law. It remains God's Word, given, as all Scripture, for our enlightenment (2 Tim. 3:16). Moreover, although the new covenant believer does not stand directly under Old Testament law, that law itself serves an important function in helping us understand our obligations. New Testament teachings are informed by the Old Testament law. For instance, the New Testament prohibits porneia—unlawful sexual conduct. But what is included in such illegitimate sexual conduct? The New Testament writers never spell it out because the scope of this conduct has been defined clearly in the Old Testament law. Thus, we continue to read the Old Testament law as a guide to our interpretation of New Testament law.

(Source: Douglas J. Moo, Romans, The NIV Application Commentary (Grand Rapids, MI: Zondervan Publishing House, 2000), 223–224.)

8

(Mis)using the Bible to Justify Race-Based Slavery

Witness here these devastating examples of Christians pastors and church institutions using Scripture to justify a horrid evil, race-based slavery.

Isaac Taylor Tichenor was the pastor of First Baptist Church of Montgomery, Alabama during the Civil War. Two years into the war, Tichenor preached an impassioned sermon to the Alabama legislature, on August 21, 1863. In that message, he sought to encourage the war-weary state that their cause was divinely inspired and that they were undoubtedly on God's side. In many ways, Dr. Tichenor's sermon is remarkable – soaked with Scripture and passion, and even a form of humility. However, underlying the whole thing is the assertion that race-based slavery is divinely "right." Here are a couple of selections from that sermon. In the first, Tichenor ends with the bold declaration that God would save the Southland, presumably from the "mad attempts of fanaticism to deprive them of their rights" (irony alert!) and overthrow the institution of African slavery. To read such a statement today is quite stunning, to say the least. In the second statement, Tichenor decries the practice of a slave owner separating a married family for economic interests, while somehow failing to realize that race-based slavery is an abominable wickedness, nowhere justified in Scripture at all.

1. Two weary years of war have wrung this question from the agonized heart of our bleeding country. "Oh! That we could have peace!" exclaims the statesman, as he ponders the problems that demand solution at his hands. "Peace," sighs the soldier, as he wraps his blanket around him and lies down to sleep upon the open field. "Peace!" moans the widow, as she reads the fatal news of her heroic husband fallen on some bloody field, and bitterly thinks of the darkened future in store for herself and her orphaned children.

77

The prayer of the land is for peace. You may hear it in the sanctuary, at the fireside, around the family altar, in the silent chamber, on the tented field. When will it come? .... If God governs the world, then his hand is in this war in which we are engaged. It matters not that the wickedness of man brought it upon us, that it was caused by the mad attempts of fanaticism to deprive us of our rights, overthrow our institutions [African slavery], and impose upon us a yoke which, as freemen, we had resolved never to bear...While the storm-cloud sweeps over our land, let us remember that God rides upon the wings of the tempest and subjects it to His will. God in His own way will save our Southland....

2. We have failed to discharge our duties to our slaves. I entertain no doubt that slavery is right, but there are abuses of it which ought to be corrected. Marriage is a divine institution, and yet marriage exists among our slaves dependent upon the will of the master. "What God has joined together, let no man put asunder," yet this tie [of marriage] is subject to the passion, caprice or avarice of their owners. The law gives the husband and the father no protection in this relation.

Both of these selections are from the book, *Isaac Taylor Tichenor, The Home Mission Statesman*, written by Jacob S. Dill and published in 1908 by the Southern Baptist Convention's Sunday School board. In the forward to the book, the author (who is a hearty admirer of Tichenor) records this verse without any sense of irony whatsoever, "*He had understanding of the times, to know what Israel ought to do.*" 1 Chronicles 12:32. Tragically, Tichenor had **zero** understanding of the times he was living in -foolishly bending and abusing Scripture to justify an abominable institution.

Ebenezer W. Warren was the pastor of the First Baptist Church of Macon Georgia, serving two terms in the 1860s and the 1880s. During his first time of service, he was a vocal supporter of the South in the Civil War, and produced sermons, pamphlets and books that sought to convince Southerners that slavery was biblical and divinely blessed by God. So committed was he to the cause of the Confederacy, that the church offered to melt down its 900 pound church bell for the purpose of being forged into a Confederate cannon. This would seem to be the very opposite of the spirit behind Isaiah 2:4, "*He will settle disputes among the nations and provide arbitration for many peoples. They will turn their swords into plows and their spears into pruning knives. Nations will not take up the sword against other nations,and they will never again train for war.*"

In January of 1861, several months before the outbreak of the Civil War, Pastor Ebenezer preached a message entitled, "Scriptural Vindication of Slavery," to a packed, standing room only, crowd at First Baptist Macon. The sermon would be printed a week later in the *Macon Telegraph*. Reproduced below is slightly less than twenty percent of that sermon. It is a long selection (and was apparently a long sermon!) but it is a very important one to read. In this sermon, Warren lays out a Divine case for race-based slavery, alleges that fighting against slavery is tantamount to fighting against God and His will, and - perhaps most troubling of all - makes the case that the enslaved blacks in the South were cheerful, happy, and defenders of slavery.

> *Some of our greatest statesmen and patriots, whose moral worth is still fragrant in the memories of all – but who better understand the laws of nations, political economy, and the Constitution of the U.S., than they did the Bible, have declared slavery to be a sin.*
> *Not a few of our standard literary and Theological works, written by Northern men of recognized learning and piety, embody a strong anti-slavery sentiment. The Sabbath school books, heretofore taught to our children; and the light literature and religious periodicals issued from the Northern presses, and read by our families, have not been free from the same pernicious and unsanctified teachings. The discourse delivered on this subject,*

whether from the pulpit or the hustings, have heretofore been by those who opposed the institution.

So frequent and declamatory have been their efforts, that a popular current of opposition has been set in commotion, which has well nigh overleaped its bounds. We of the South have been passive, hoping the storm would subside and leave the wrecks of its own folly and madness upon the field that gave it birth. Our passiveness has been our sin. We have not come up to the vindication of God and of truth, as duty demanded. The consequence has been, as might have been expected. A few of our own people have been prepared to look upon slavery as a "necessary evil." Some others are unsettled in their views, and apologize for, rather than justify the institution. While many who believe it is right, have not taken the time to investigate it thoroughly as it is taught from Heaven – and hence, are better prepared to defend it upon constitutional, than upon Bible grounds.

For these reasons, it is necessary for ministers of the Gospel ... to teach slavery from the pulpit, as it was taught by the holy men of old, who spake as moved by the Holy Spirit. I should feel I was derelict to my religious obligations to God – wanting in philanthropy to the negro race among us – and unfaithful to the high, social and religious interest of my State, were I, at this crisis, to decline, as a religious teacher, to give my congregation what I conceive to be the revealed word of God on this subject.

Both Christianity and Slavery are from Heaven; both are blessings to humanity; both are to be perpetuated to the end of time; and therefore both have been protected and defended by God's omnipotent arm from the assaults, oppositions and persecutions through which they have passed.

Why are our slaves still peaceful and happy, notwithstanding the incendiary spirit of abolitionism? Why have they not revolted and thrown off the yoke of bondage? Why do hundreds go forth at the will of one man, to their daily labor, contented and happy?

Why to we hear their merry laugh and cheerful songs, and see their sports of mirth – giving evidences, of joyous and happy hearts, and that, too, while they are as conscious as we are that they are held in involuntary servitude? Because Slavery is right; and because the condition of the slaves affords them all those privileges which would prove substantial blessings to them; and, too, because their Maker has decreed their bondage, and has given them, as a race, capacities and aspirations suited alone to this condition of life.

Refer to these as Signs of the Times, which show that Providence instead of releasing the negro from bondage, is raising up faithful and gifted men among them, to defend the institution which enslaves them. I challenge the world to produce another instance, in which the enslaved, of any land, have believed it to be morally and religiously right to be held in bondage, and have, on principle, come to the defense of those who held them in bondage. The hand of God was not more obvious in the release of the Israelites from bondage, than it is apparent, in enslaving the Africans who are among us.

I desire to meet one plausible, but specious objection to slavery, urged by the abolitionists before I take my seat.

It is said that one single passage in the gospel, imperatively requires every master at once to emancipate his slaves. It is recorded in Mat. 7:12. "Therefore, all things whatsoever ye would that men should do to you, do ye even so to them, for this is the law and the prophets." It is thought, that if the master would desire liberty, were he a slave, he is bound by this rule, to liberate his slave. But his argument is specious, and this construction, if applied to the various relations of life will subvert all the laws and regulations of society and governments. A criminal is arraigned, tried and found guilty of a violation of the law – but the judge would not desire to be punished were he in the criminal's place – is he bound therefore to release him? .... A desire entertained by a servant to be set at liberty, is an unlawful desire, because its accomplishment, would violate the "law" which enjoins perpetual servitude. Christianity has had her trials, and is now in some measure, enjoying her triumph. Slavery is her trial now, but a triumph, which shall honor God, and bless humanity awaits her in the future.

The ignorance that is on display here in this message is enough to make the blood boil. There is so much scriptural twisting, so much eisegesis, so many wrong assumptions, and a fury-inducing tendency to capitalize the word "slavery." Warren's 'sermon,' and I use that word with a shudder in this case, reminds me of this civil rights era picture, and the unvarnished ignorance it portrays:

Notice how proud they look of their silly sign, oblivious to the fact that it is sealing the back door shut.

Another thing that gives me a shudder is the historical description of Ebenezer Warren on the *current* web page of First Baptist church of Macon.

> *Ebenezer W. Warren, our church's longest-serving pastor, served tenures in the 1860s and 1880s. The defining event of Warren's first pastorate was the Civil War. In January, 1861 Warren preached a memorable sermon in support of slavery.Warren played a crucial role in moving Mercer University to Macon in 1870. In the 1880s, he served as Chair of the Executive Committee of the Georgia Baptist Convention. The Warren Memorial Hospital in China, funded by our church, was the first Southern Baptist hospital constructed on foreign soil, It was named in honor of Warren. Despite his short-sightedness on the issue of slavery, Dr. Warren was deeply respected among the people of Macon for his character, gentleness, sincerity, and acts of goodness. He left a significant legacy in the history of our church. (Source: http://fbcxmacon.squarespace.com/pastor-history/ 2011/8/14/ebenezer-w-warren-1860-1871-1879-1891.html)*

I'm not one to normally get up in arms about things found on the internet, but I find it really quite surprising that Warren, a seditious racist who pushed the country towards war and destruction, is remembered so fondly. Warren's position on slavery and race was far worse than mere "short-sightedness." It was damnable heresy.

Speaking of the Southern Baptists, in May of 1863 the South Carolina convention of Southern Baptists passed a resolution that was intended to denounce the idea that some Southern Christians were wavering in their support for slavery. In that resolution, one finds the following:

> *"The war which has been forced upon us by our assailants, is*

grounded in opposition to an institution which is sustained by the sanctions of religion. **They assume that slavery is a sin and therefore ought to be abolished. We contend that it is a Scriptural institution.** *The very nature of the contest takes the point in dispute out of the category of politics, and delegates it to the sphere of Christianity.* **We are really contending for the precepts of religion, against the devices of the wisdom of this world,** *and it is, therefore, not only the policy, but the duty of religious bodies to define their position in this great contest. The convention has done well in giving unambiguous utterance to its sentiments on this subject."*

See clearly how the statement clearly contends that their form of slavery was scriptural, but never gives any sort of Scripture to back up that particular point. And, just so that we understand that racism was not merely a thing in the 1800s, here is former Democratic senator Robert Byrd, the longest serving Senator in U.S. History (who died in office in 2010) writing a protest letter to his own senator at the time of World War 2:

"I shall never fight in the armed forces with a negro by my side ... Rather I should die a thousand times, and see Old Glory trampled in the dirt never to rise again, than to see this beloved land of ours become degraded by race mongrels, a throwback to the blackest specimen from the wilds. Robert Byrd letter to Theodore Bilbo, 1944. It is important to note that he later disavowed those words and his founding of a chapter of the KKK.

One final historical record of note should be mentioned, as it is in a class by itself in terms of frenzied rhetoric and biblical gymnastics.

One might think that there are too many examples of 'Christians' justifying racism here, but my response to that would be that modern white evangelical Christians need to fully apprehend the levels to which our evangelical forbears would go to in order to try and justify their sinful behavior. We will not understand the uneasiness, fear and distrust of our black brothers and sisters, until we understand these deceptions here that have logically led to those apprehensions, fears and distrust. The paragraph below is from a religious screed, published by the Virginia Baptists in 1864. It seeks to make the case that those who are seeking to abolish slavery are, in fact, the final Antichrist. (and no, I am not kidding.)

> *This seems obvious. And then, does not humanitarianism—this gem of the last and crowning mystery of iniquity—everywhere voice itself in anti-slaveryism! Is not abolitionism, therefore, (to say no more,) the point of transition, for the present age, to that "apotheosis of man"—first, of man's nature, next of individual man—which shall constitute "the final Antichrist!" And in fighting against Abolitionism are we not fighting against "the final Antichrist,"—at least in the shape of the principle which goes before and prepares the way for him! Have we no need to be a purified people, that we may worthily wage such a war? Should not faith and prayer rank among our chosen weapons? Should we not seek to be "full of power, and of judgment, and of might, through the Spirit of the Lord?" Will not God eventually make bare His arm on our behalf, though He long subjects us to the fiery purgation of battle and blockade, fitting us for the position of triumphant championship to the cause which is more His own than ours? (Source: "Abolition: The Final Antichrist." The Religious Herald of the Virginia Baptists, January 14, 1864.)*

Speaking frankly, I read the above statements by Christians trying to justify an abomination (race-based slavery) and it enrages me.

It is such an abuse of the Bible, and such a failure to understand the good news of Jesus, not to mention about two or three dozen other critical doctrines of Scripture. These pastors, and their stupid, godless rhetoric, are at least somewhat to blame for the Civil War in America and the devastating amount of deaths that happened in those few years. According to the New York Times, many historians are now estimating that 750,000 Americans died during the Civil War, a 20 percent increase from previous estimates. (Source: www.ny-times.com/2012/04/03/

science/civil-war-toll-up-by-20-percent-in-new-estimate.html)

That means roughly 2.5 percent of Americans died during the Civil War. To put that figure into perspective, the number of Americans who died in EVERY OTHER WAR **PUT TOGETHER** is 644,000. And the men quoted above, all of those influential leaders and preachers during the Civil War? They have blood on their hands. They lied about God and His Word. They believed that race-based slavery was not only acceptable, but that it was God-demanded. That it was worth fighting AND KILLING for. They were dead wrong, and their level of wrongness produced countless orphans and widows, and an unimaginable level of unnecessary suffering in this country. Bad theology, stubbornly adhered to, is deadly and damning.

When I consider the cruelty that this nation has demonstrated towards black people, I understand former San Francisco 49ers quarterback Colin Kaepernick's frustration a little better. I understand why Philadelphia Eagles safety Malcolm Jenkins raises his fist during the national anthem, as a silent sort of protest. I'm actually glad that a white guy like Chris Long would come over and put his arm around Jenkins (in a show of unity) while Jenkins was protesting. Please understand – I stand during the national anthem. When we are at home watching a football game on TV, I even ask my kids to stand up. I want them to respect our country and our flag.

While I believe the best and most unifying way forward for black brothers and sisters in this country is to not protest the flag or the anthem, I still understand why Kaepernick and Jenkins and others might struggle with that, and I would never attempt to correct them for doing so. I simply cannot wrap my mind around an understanding of what it must be like to be black in a country that was cruel to blacks for centuries. Before you rant and rave on social media about that, perhaps you should try and consider things from their perspective, and maybe ask some hard questions.

How would I react in that situation? Would I protest like Kaepernick and Jenkins? Maybe so. I'd like to think I would be courageous, at the very least, and speak truth to power in the most Christ-honoring way possible. Our country was terrible to people like Jenkins and Kaepernick (and whomever) for hundreds of years, and we probably shouldn't be surprised that it might take more than a few decades of uneasy renunciations by whites of the ways of the past, for our black brothers and sisters to be more comfortable respecting the flag and the anthem. Thabiti Anyabwile is a writer for the Gospel Coalition that I greatly respect. During the 2016 election, he wrote the paragraph below, which contains concepts that white evangelicals need to grasp immediately, if they have not already done so.

> *Here's the problem with living 50 years after the American Civil Rights Movement and the de jure segregation of the land that produced it: Too many people now have no idea how every-day-horrendous-and-perilous life was under that system. (Source: https://blogs.thegospelcoalition.org/thabitianyabwile/)*

Can you be a Christian and a bond-servant owner? Puzzleingly, the answer to that question is an unequivocal yes. While I am not crazy about that affirmative answer, the fact of the matter is that in Scripture, we have the curious case of a Christian bond-servant owner. His name was Philemon, and Paul called him a brother, even as he urged him to set his bond-servant, Onesimus, free. At least we know that it was possible for one bond-servant owner to be a Christian.

What about some of the above named preachers during the Civil War, those that advocated for race-based slavery, in a most passionate and horrific way. Could those people be Christians? The answer to that question is essentially above my pay grade. We might think that it would be impossible for them to be saved by Jesus, because their sin was far too horrific. But it is worth realizing that my own sin also is far too horrific for me to be a candidate for salvation also; in fact it's an abomination.

Your sin almost certainly is also. I believe one of the reasons why there was such a spike in social media posts condemning racism and what happened in Charlottesville is the fact that we almost all agree that white supremacy is an evil far beyond most of our ability to commit. I think the fact of the matter is, that there are few legitimate white supremacists in America. And when I say few, I mean less than 10% of the population. Which I recognize, of course, represents a higher number than we should like. I merely mean that true white supremacists, the kind that will march and be vocal, are in the minority. Racists of every stripe, however, are much more prevalent.

It is easy for us to judge the slaveholders of the Southern states in the 1800s. and there are good reasons for that ease. However, and let me first say this as loudly and clearly as possible, their sin of racism and race-based slavery was incredibly foul, soaked in unwarranted pride, and without excuse. I abominate it, and I abominate the kind of conscience that could commit such a thing in an ongoing way and still claim to be a follower of Jesus. However, the fact of the matter is, there is probably other kinds of sin of a similarly abominable nature in my life or in the lives of some of the people reading this. "We have all sinned and fallen short of the glory of God." Thus when we condemn racism on Facebook, let us do it aware that, there but for the grace of God, go we. Don't "feel good" about condemning racism in others, rather grieve that racism is still prevalent in our society, and lovingly (but firmly) seek the repentance of those who are giving vent to such vileness.

One other note, before we move on. Some might argue that that the above quoted pastors and leaders were merely "products of their time," and there might be some small truth to the assertion. Christians, however, have zero excuse for racism, because the Bible has zero tolerance for it, and contains volumes of discourse opposed to racism in any form. It might be helpful to understand that Southern Christian pastors weren't the only racists active during the 1800s. Scientific darling Charles Darwin also wrote many troubling passages that would be deemed horribly offensive by moderns. Some examples of such passages (which are the very definition of pseudoscience) are:

> *Slavery, although in some ways beneficial during ancient times, is a great crime; yet it was not so regarded until quite recently, even by the most civilised nations. And this was especially the case,because the slaves belonged in general to a race different from that of their masters. As barbarians do not regard the opinion of their women, wives are commonly treated like slaves. Most savages are utterly indifferent to the sufferings of strangers, or even delight in witnessing them. It is well known that the women and children of the North American Indians aided in torturing their enemies. Some savages take a horrid pleasure in cruelty to animals, and humanity is an unknown virtue. Nevertheless, besides the family affections, kindness is common, especially during sickness, between the members of the same tribe, and is sometimes extended beyond these limits. Mungo Park's touching account of the kindness of the negro women of the interior to him is well known. Many instances could be given of the noble fidelity of savages towards each other, but not to strangers; common experience justifies the maxim of the Spaniard, "Never, never trust an Indian."*
> *The great break in the organic chain between man and his nearest*

allies, which cannot be bridged over by any extinct or living species, has often been advanced as a grave objection to the belief that man is descended from some lower form; but this objection will not appear of much weight to those who, from general reasons, believe in the general principle of evolution. Breaks often occur in all parts of the series, some being wide, sharp and defined, others less so in various degrees; as between the orang and its nearest allies– between the Tarsius and the other Lemuridae– between the elephant, and in a more striking manner between the Ornithorhynchus or Echidna, and all other mammals. But these breaks depend merely on the number of related forms which have become extinct. At some future period, not very distant as measured by centuries, the civilised races of man will almost certainly exterminate, and replace, the savage races throughout the world.

At the same time the anthropomorphous apes, as Professor Schaaffhausen has remarked, will no doubt be exterminated. The break between man and his nearest allies will then be wider, for it will intervene between man in a more civilised state, as we may hope, even than the Caucasian, and some ape as low as a baboon, instead of as now between the negro or Australian and the gorilla. (Source: Charles Darwin, The Descent of Man, p. 81, 1871)

I count at least seven passages in these few paragraphs of Darwin's that are egregiously racist and intolerable: *Slavery had its benefits, slaves were of a different race than their master, never trust an Indian!, some 'savages' are completely heartless and utterly cruel. civilized people will one day exterminate the savages. Australians and 'negroes' are closer to the apes than Caucasians.* These statements are just utterly awful, and they are supposedly based in science. It would do moderns well to remember that our ancestors – the scientists, the pastors and the statesmen, were often blind to their foul racism. Perhaps we are blind too, and thus we should be careful and humble and vigilant.

9

Slaves of Christ and the Biblical Key to Greatness

"The Greatest among you will be your servant."

Phil 1:1 *Opens this way: "Paul and Timothy, servants of Christ Jesus."* The word that Paul uses there is, of course, our word "*dou-*

los/servant/slave" Paul opens the majestic book of Philippians with the unmistakable claim that he is a *doulos*/servant/slave of Christ, and so is Timothy. As noted previously, Paul designates himself as a *doulos*/servant/slave multiple times, which gives us a very strong indication of how the Bible views being in that position. The fact is, the New Testament understanding of one who is in the position of *doulos*/servant/slave is very high.

As also discussed earlier, the first century word '*doulos*' represents a position that is not quite as high as a servant or butler in the American-European way of thinking, but probably a good bit higher than what we think of when we envision the word 'slave.' As such, for this chapter, I am going to use the term "bond-servant," because I think it probably represents the best translation and meaning for *doulos*.

When I was first starting out in ministry as a youth pastor, some other youth pastor friends and I created a company called "Doulos Services." You could hire Doulos services to cut your grass, paint your offices, move your furniture to Michigan, re-roof your house, haul stuff to the dump, design your website, or clean up your yard. As *doulois* for Christ, me and my fellow youth pastors did all of those jobs, literally, and more beside. It was not easy work, and gave each of us a taste – a small taste – of what it might have been like to have been a first century *doulos*.

Over and over again, Christians are called bond-servants in Scripture – bond-servants of God, bond-servants of Jesus. To understand why the the New Testament doesn't outright ban the existence of the bond-servant, or *doulos*, and even commands bond-servants to obey their masters and do well for them – you have to understand the reality that being a bond-servant and serving is a great thing in the eyes of Jesus. Consider these Scriptures:

1. Acts 2:18 prophesies that God is going to pour out His Spirit on his bond-servants at the end of days, and they will boldly prophesy.

2. In Acts 4:29-30 we see that the church is called a bond-servant, and that Jesus Himself is a servant (*pais*): *"Now, Lord, consider their threats and enable your <u>servants</u> to speak your word with great boldness. 30 Stretch out your hand to heal and perform miraculous signs and wonders through the name of your holy <u>servant</u> Jesus."*

3. Angels are bond-servants: In Revelation 19, John receives an exceedingly great prophetic revelation from an angel. John is so overwhelmed by the encounter, that he bows down prostrate, and begins to worship, but the angel quickly makes him stop, because the angel himself is merely a fellow bond-servant of Jesus:

> *And the angel said to me, "Write this: Blessed are those who are invited to the marriage supper of the Lamb." And he said to me, "These are the true words of God." 10 Then I fell down at his feet to worship him, but he said to me, "You must not do that! <u>I am a fellow servant with you and your brothers</u> who hold to the testimony of Jesus. Worship God." For the testimony of Jesus is the spirit of prophecy. Revelation 19:9-10, ESV*

4. Consider this fascinating passage from Paul in 1 Corinthians 7, in which he urges bond-servants to get their freedom if they are able, and tells those Christians that are not bond-servants of people that they are still bond-servants of Christ:

> *Were you a bond-servant when called? Do not be concerned about it. (But if you can gain your freedom, avail yourself of the opportunity.) 22 For he who was called in the Lord as a bond-servant is a freedman of the Lord. Likewise he who was free when called is a bond-servant of Christ. 23 You were bought with a price; do not become bond-servants of men. (1 Corinthians 7:21-23)*

It is thus clear that being a bond-servant, in the eyes of Jesus and the writers of the New Testament, was not a necessarily a bad thing. **To repeat our conclusions from the last chapters, race-based slavery IS A BAD and WICKED EVIL, and its purveyors are without excuse for their crimes against God's Word.** But the *doulos* system of the first century was not that. And in wrestling with the question of why the New Testament still permits the existence of the *doulos* system, we have to realize that Jesus not only doesn't look down on serving and being a bond-servant, He actually glorifies the position, and calls it the path to eternal greatness in this pericope from Mark 9:

> *And they came to Capernaum. And when he was in the house he asked them, "What were you discussing on the way?" 34 But they kept silent, for on the way they had argued with one another about who was the greatest. 35 And he sat down and called the twelve. And he said to them, "If anyone would be first, he must be last of all and servant of all." 36 And he took a child and put him in the midst of them, and taking him in his arms, he said to them, 37 "Whoever receives one such child in my name receives me, and whoever receives me, receives not me but him who sent me." (Mark 9:33-37, ESV)*

Servant-greatness is one of the most underrated and underappreciated key themes of the Bible. Whenever I see a very gifted person serving in a menial sort of way, I always think to myself, "Ah-hah! That person understands the key to greatness." When I see a gifted person operating in his or her gifts and intentionally NOT serving in any menial way, I wonder if they've understood the teaching of Jesus that those who would be first/leaders must place themselves last, and ultimately serve everybody else. The greatest pastors, leaders, and teachers in the church must always serve. In Mark 10, we can see this teaching of Jesus driven home even deeper. Considering that this episode came directly on the heels of an eerily similar situation in Mark 9, I adjudge that most Christians today need multiple reminders that the way of Jesus is a way of serving and sacrifice:

> *And James and John, the sons of Zebedee, came up to him and said to him, "Teacher, we want you to do for us whatever we ask of you." 36 And he said to them, "What do you want me to do for you?" 37 And they said to him, "Grant us to sit, one at your right hand and one at your left, in your glory." 38 Jesus said to them, "You do not know what you are asking. Are you able to drink the cup that I drink, or to be baptized with the baptism with which I am baptized?" 39 And they said to him, "We are able." And Jesus said to them, "The cup that I drink you will drink, and with the baptism with which I am baptized, you will be baptized, 40 but to sit at my right hand or at my left is not mine to grant, but it is for those for whom it has been prepared."*
>
> *And when the ten heard it, they began to be indignant at James and John. 42 And Jesus called them to him and said to them, "You know that those who are considered rulers of the Gentiles lord it over them, and their great ones exercise authority over them. 43 But it shall not be so among you. But whoever would be great among you must be your servant, 44 and whoever would be first among you must be slave of all. 45 For even the Son of Man came not to be served but to serve, and to give his life as a ransom for many. (Mark 10:34-45, ESV)*

Notice something remarkably important: James and John weren't rebuked for wanting to be great, but for not realizing that the pathway to greatness was suffering and serving. Jesus gives Himself as an example: even He came to serve, and not be served. If you are reading this, and you wish to be great, then by all means – pursue it! Don't be falsely humble, but do remember that the path to greatness in the Kingdom of God is to reckon yourself last, and serve everybody else.

To repeat, for one to understand why the New Testament doesn't outlaw bond-servants, one must understand that Jesus had an incredibly high view of serving others, and being a bond-servant. When I ponder this truth, I consider Karl Marx's famous claim that "Religion is the opium of the people." I agree with him, in part. Man-made religion really is designed to be a sort of drug, meant to soothe the soul, and kill pain, without effecting any curative or healing powers whatsoever. That's what opium does – it makes you *feel* better, but it doesn't help. Following Jesus isn't like that at all. Considering His call to serve (and His promise of tribulation in John 16:33), following Jesus is anything but a pain-killer. Following Jesus is more like a pain-inviter, but it is also an eternal life bringer. Ultimately.

The Kingdom of Jesus is an upside-down Kingdom, and if church history is any indication, we haven't understood His teachings on this subject very well. The way to prominence in the Kingdom of Jesus is to serve everybody, and to be last – even titles are to be avoided, because the exaltation of self is not at all to be desired. Read Matthew 23 here, and think about how many Christian leaders have missed these incredibly clear commands of Jesus. Have we too missed them?

Then Jesus said to the crowds and to his disciples, 2 "The scribes and the Pharisees sit on Moses' seat, 3 so do and observe whatever they tell you, but not the works they do. For they preach, but do not practice. 4 They tie up heavy burdens, hard to bear, and lay them on people's shoulders, but they themselves are not willing to move them with their finger. 5 They do all their deeds to be seen by others. For they make their phylacteries broad and their fringes long, 6 and they love the place of honor at feasts and the best seats in the synagogues 7 and greetings in the marketplaces and being called rabbi by others. 8 But you are not to be called rabbi, for you have one teacher, and you are all brothers. 9 And call no man your father on earth, for you have one Father, who is in heaven. 10 Neither be called instructors, for you have one instructor, the Christ. 11 The greatest among you shall be your servant. 12 Whoever exalts himself will be humbled, and whoever humbles himself will be exalted. (Matthew 23:1-12, ESV)

This is a core teaching of Jesus - don't take titles for yourself! Don't exalt yourself! Don't put yourself first! Do serve others! Do humble yourself! Do make yourself last of all! At least six times in Scripture, Jesus identifies servanthood as THE key to greatness. When we understand this dynamic, we can then begin to understand the New Testament teaching on being a bond-servant. **The Bible is adamantly against any sort of racism, or race based slavery. The preachers of the Confederacy, and today's supporters of Confederate ideals are dead wrong on that**. But, the Bible doesn't condemn the non-racial practice of being a bond-servant, or even having a bond-servant, because the Bible has such a high view of the call to serve. *(If you are thinking about somehow having a bond-servant, simply because the Bible doesn't outright condemn the practice, let me hit you with the implications of Jesus' above teaching on service: In the Kingdom of Heaven, the last shall be FIRST, and many who are first, will be last. Since the Kingdom of Heaven is eternal, it is foolishness in the extreme to spend your life being served, considering such a life is likely to lead to being last - eternally! - in the Kingdom of Heaven. Why trade away a few moments of pleasure and ease for an eternity of being...last?)*

Why does the Bible have such a high view of serving? I'll offer two reasons. The first is that human beings are made in the Image of God, and they are thus immortal. As immortal beings, the 70 or so years that humans live on earth are a mere drop in the ocean of the existence of man. According to Jesus, the vast majority of that existence will either be with Him in eternal life, or apart from Him in eternal punishment. (See Matthew 25:46) Therefore, we are living for eternity, and Jesus says that serving on Earth will yield eternal rewards. From God's perspective, our time of living on Earth is but a vapor, and if that time is spent serving others, no great injustice has been done, since that service will yield a harvest of eternal greatness. Serving is good, and serving carries with it eternal rewards.

- Secondly, the Bible has such a high view of service because Jesus Himself – the KING OF KINGS – became a servant. As unbelievable as it is, the book of Philippians tells us that Jesus the Master became a *doulos*. And considering that Christians are not greater than our master – we must also be a doulos to others, whether that is our job, or our free privilege.

Therefore if you have any encouragement from being united with Christ, if any comfort from his love, if any common sharing in the Spirit, if any tenderness and compassion, 2 then make my joy complete by being like-minded, having the same love, being one in spirit and of one mind. 3 Do nothing out of selfish ambition or vain conceit. Rather, in humility value others above yourselves, 4 not looking to your own interests but each of you to the interests of the others.5 In your relationships with one another, have the same mindset as Christ Jesus:6 Who, being in very nature God, did not consider equality with God something to be used to his own advantage; 7 rather, he made himself nothing by taking the very nature of a servant, (Doulos – SLAVE/BONDSERVANT) being made in human likeness. 8 And being found in appearance as a man, he humbled himself by becoming obedient to death—even death on a cross! 9 Therefore God exalted him to the highest place and gave him the name that is above every name,10 that at the name of Jesus every knee should bow, in heaven and on earth and under the earth, 11 and every tongue acknowledge that Jesus Christ is Lord, to the glory of God the Father. (Philippians 2:1-12)

10

Was Jesus White?

Jesus, as depicted in the Lumo Project film "The Gospel of John."

No.

What...just a simple one word answer isn't good enough for you?

The truth of it is that Jesus wasn't exactly white, nor was He precisely black either. He was, most likely, in the middle! Ultimately, the question of "whiteness" is a difficult and awkward question to ask and answer for anybody, much less a historical figure, from a disputed part of the world. In the past, the United States largely considered Middle Easterners as non-white, but things changed, at least on an official level, as the result of a court case in 1909. Sadly, the case was ignited and surrounded by a substantial amount of racism.

Officer George Shishim was a Lebanese-American police officer in Los Angeles County in the 1900s. In 1909, he arrested the white son of a prominent L.A. attorney for disturbing the peace. That a 'yellow-skinned' foreigner had arrested his sin didn't sit well with this attorney, and he sued the county, claiming that, as officer Shishim was Lebanese, that meant he was not white, but Chinese-Mongolian, and thus ineligible for citizenship in America. How a white attorney at the time came to characterize a Lebanese man as "Chinese-Mongolian" has a little bit to do with the conquerings of Genghis Khan, and a whole lot to do with plain old ignorant racism. The case would appear before Los Angeles Country Judge Hutton, and the federal government argued against the potential citizenship of Shisham, declaring that as a Middle-Easterner, he was not white, and thus not eligible for citizenship.

Shisham's defense, however, was an absolute stroke of genius. He argued to the court, who largely identified as Christian, that, "If I am a Mongolian, then so was Jesus, because we came from the same land." This proved to be a persuasive argument to Judge Hutton, who announced his decision the following day:

This is an application by one George Shishim, a Syrian, to be admitted to citizenship. The federal government, acting through the department of justice, objects to his admission, basing its objection on the sole ground that he is not a member of the white race in contemplation of section 2169 of the revised statutes of the

*United States. (Source: http://www.arabamericanhistory.org/
archives/dept-of-justice-affirms-arab-race-in-1909/)*

And thus it was that Middle-Easterners, including Israelis, came to be considered "white." by the United States government, largely against its will. Interestingly, there is a movement underway to overturn this designation, and it is likely that by the next census, 'MENA' will be a new designation, standing for "Middle East or North Africa."

Just last week I posted a mock up of the cover for this book on my Facebook page. I included a two word description of the picture that said "current project," and nothing else. That post has become one of the most controversial posts I've ever made on Facebook. It generated lots of likes and nearly 150 comments, which is a fairly high number for one of my posts. The reason for that many comments is that within about 15 minutes of posting the picture, one of my Facebook 'friends,' I lady I've never met before and actually don't even know in real life, posted an excerpt from the book of Deuteronomy in response to my picture.

I read the excerpt with some degree of curiosity trying to discern what her comment meant, it had no context other than the verse itself, Deuteronomy 7:3, which is a prohibition that was aimed at the Israelites commanding them to not marry foreign wives in the promised land. For years, racists and people who have utterly misunderstood the Bible, have used that passage (and others like it) to decry interracial marriage, interracial relationships and those sorts of things.

Reading Deuteronomy 7 as a current prohibition against Christians marrying somebody of a different nationality or skin color is a tragic misunderstanding of Scripture that completely disregards who the Old Testament was written to and the context of those commandments in Deuteronomy.

Deuteronomy 7:3-6 **Do not intermarry with them. Do not give** *your daughters to their sons or take their daughters for your sons, 4 because they will turn your sons away from Me to worship other gods. Then the Lord's anger will burn against you, and He will swiftly destroy you. 5 Instead, this is what you are to do to them: tear down their altars, smash their sacred pillars, cut down their Asherah poles, and burn up their carved images. 6 For you are a holy people belonging to the Lord your God. The Lord your God has chosen you to be His own possession out of all the peoples on the face of the earth.*

The Jews were not allowed to intermarry with foreigners not because of the color of their skin but very clearly because of their religion. By this command, God sought to keep the hearts of the Israelites pure and their worship focused solely on Him, in keeping with the first commandment, "Do not have other gods besides Me." It had nothing to do with keeping their blood pure.

Suspicious of the post, and wondering why she chose to post that particular Scripture, I went to check out my "'friend's' Facebook page and discovered a trove of highly racist memes, racist comments and claims, and other highly offensive and inaccurate material including the picture you see below, which alleges that the Bible is only about white people , that Adam was a white person and that any attempt to describe the Bible as a book about mixed races is completely false.

The Word Adam is translated from a Hebrew word "aw-damn" or "aw-dam." (#119 and #120 in Strong's Concordance) The word "Adam" means "RUDDY" (#120), "TO SHOW BLOOD (in the face), FLUSH OR TURN ROSY, BE (made) RED (ruddy)." This clearly shows, the Hebrew meaning of the word "ADAM" identifies him as a WHITE MAN. Adam was ruddy...he could blush...he could show blood in the face. Adam was the beginning of the White Race upon this earth.

Therefore, the Holy Bible is the History of the White Race; Later to become known as "ANGLO-SAXONS" after Isaac as the Scriptures relate. For God said:

"...IN ISAAC SHALL THY SEED BE CALLED." (Genesis 21:12)

"And the Lord spake unto Moses, saying...AND THEY [children of Israel and others] SHALL PUT MY NAME [CHRIST - ian] UPON THE CHILDREN OF ISRAEL; and I will bless them." (Numbers 6:22, 27)

THE BIBLE IS NOT THE HISTORY OF ANY OTHER RACE, AND ANYONE SEEKING TO MAKE THE BIBLE A MULTI-RACIAL BOOK, IS TEACH-ING DOCTRINE CONTRARY TO WHAT THE BIBLE ITSELF TEACH-ES.

Racist Claptrap!

I was incensed, disgusted and deeply troubled at the level of false teaching she was promulgating and therefore I challenged her comment on my Facebook page with some degree of firmness. This, as you might imagine, ignited one of those comment wars that are becoming more and more common on social media, as she apparently tagged in several of her white nationalist racist friends and without any effort on my part several of my friends joined in and for a while it was a free-for-all.

Her primary henchmen, and I think that is an appropriate word for the situation, was a German Nazi white supremacist that claimed to love the Jews. (Yes, it was a very strange conversation.) In fact the first commenter herself claimed to be a Jewish person despite the fact that she was quite clearly a southern American. This was a new flavor of racism for me and upon a little bit of research I discovered that there was quite a few people who make the claim that the Israelites were white, Adam was white, Jesus was white, and that the only race that is eligible for salvation is the white race. According to these white supremacists' abominable teachings, no other race is eligible for salvation. The Bible is about white people and was only written to white people. Thus according to my 'friend's' henchman, racism is actually a kindness and displays love, because it's communicating the will of God.

What a disgusting and horrific idea! But it does at least raise an interesting question and that question is what color was Jesus? Many people have in their mind this view of Jesus as a lithe white man with long hair. The trouble with this picture of Jesus is that it comes from the Italian Renaissance, where the Italian painters initially depicted Jesus as somebody very similar to them, with long hair (as was the fashion in that day), slightly tanned skin, and usually a white robe. The only part of that depiction that has some basis in reality is the robe. The fact is, we have no surviving pictures of Jesus from His time. In fact the earliest surviving picture we have that depicts Jesus is copied below, dates from the 200s, and obviously doesn't show details about the race of Jesus or much about His appearance or anything like that. One of the other earliest depictions of Jesus dates from the 300s AD, and is a picture with quite a bit more detail present in the facial area. Surprisingly, for some, this second picture does appear to show Jesus as a dark-skinned man.

The Good Shepherd fresco, from the St. Callisto Catacomb in Rome, circa 200s AD.

*Detail from "Christ Between Peter and Paul," a painting found in a Roman
cemetery that dates to the 300s AD. Note the dark skin of Jesus!*

The pictures above are not definitive, however what we do know is that Jesus was in Israel and the Bible never describes Him in a way that would particularly distinguish Him from the rest of His race. For instance, Jesus is never described as being particularly tall, fat, balding, redheaded etc., Therefore it is quite reasonable to conclude that Jesus probably looked much like the other Israelite men of His day.

So, what did the Israelites look like? Are Israelites white? The fact of the matter is that the Israelites are a Middle-Eastern people with a great amount of variety within their borders just like Americans, Asians and Africans have a great amount of variety among their peoples. If you were asked to describe a typical American, that might be somewhat difficult, given the wide variety of peoples in America. Nevertheless, it is possible to engage in some small amount of description of the average Israelite, and therefore to give a pretty good facsimile representation of what Jesus probably looked like. In recent times, Scientists have actually done this through skeletal remains, and reconstructed a picture and description of what the average Isrealite, and therefore Jesus, could have looked like. That reconstruction depicts Jesus as a man with olive/brown skin, black and short hair, and a heavy black beard. It isn't exactly a picture of the historical Jesus, but it is a scientific representation of what the average Israelite person would look like.

Some might be surprised that Jesus didn't have long hair, but the only men who had long hair in first century Israel were those who had taken a Nazirite vow (and some foreigners.) We know that Jesus probably didn't have long hair because the apostle Paul wrote that it was shameful for men to have long hair, and, as Paul saw Jesus on the Damascus Road, it is highly unlikely that Jesus had the sort of long hair that is depicted of him in most pictures. If the scientific reconstruction of first century Israelites is accurate, then Jesus would be neither black nor white, but somewhere in between.

What difference does it make? The problem with this discussion is that "whiteness" is a relative term and it's not a very helpful one. People don't genuinely have white skin – an actual white-skinned person would be awfully strange looking. People that are Caucasian generally have a peach/pinkish tone to their skin, and I'm not really sure how that came to be referred to as white, but as we've seen in earlier chapters, true white skin is considered diseased skin. The funny thing about "whiteness" is the fact that most people in the white community generally consider paleness to be a less than attractive feature. In fact, in the United States of America, many people pay good money to lie in coffin-like light booths, so that ultraviolet lamps might turn their skin a few shades darker, because in their mind, darker skin on a white person looks more attractive. What a strange set of circumstances!

One more thing that is worth considering. Whether Jesus _was_ white or black on earth is not really important now, because He doesn't actually look like He used to anymore. If we were to see Jesus now, we would see His glorified body, and the biblical description of Jesus' glorified body is quite astounding. Consider the following:

> Then I turned to see the voice that was speaking to me, and on turning I saw seven golden lampstands, 13 and in the midst of the lampstands one like a son of man, clothed with a long robe and with a golden sash around his chest. 14 The hairs of his head were white, like white wool, like snow. His eyes were like a flame of fire, 15 his feet were like burnished bronze, refined in a furnace, and his voice was like the roar of many waters. 16 In his right hand he held seven stars, from his mouth came a sharp two-edged sword, and his face was like the sun shining in full strength.
> 17 When I saw him, I fell at his feet as though dead. But he laid his right hand on me, saying, "Fear not, I am the first and the last, 18 and the living one. I died, and behold I am alive forevermore, and I have the keys of Death and Hades. 19 Write therefore the things

that you have seen, those that are and those that are to take place after this. 20 As for the mystery of the seven stars that you saw in my right hand, and the seven golden lampstands, the seven stars are the angels of the seven churches, and the seven lampstands are the seven churches. Revelation 1:12-20 ESV

I deduce from John's description here in Revelation 1 that Jesus is no longer olive-skinned. He is, first and foremost, terrifying and awe-inspiring to the point that John, who leaned his head on Jesus' chest at the Last Supper, takes one look at Him here and passes out from sheer horror. As to skin color, He has the appearance of "polished bronze," which is a gleaming metallic color that is somewhere between the 'yellowness' of brass and the 'orangeness' of copper. Perhaps you can take some level of pride in the color of your skin if it has a metallic, polished bronze appearance, but I don't really know of any humans who look like that.

11

On Earth as in Heaven - Segregated Churches?

Segregationist Bob Jones Sr. Preaching

After this I looked, and behold, a great multitude that no one could number, from every nation, from all tribes and peoples and languages, standing before the throne and before the Lamb, clothed in white robes, with palm branches in their hands, 10 and crying out with a loud voice, "Salvation belongs to our God who sits on the throne, and to the Lamb!"11 And all the angels were standing around the throne and around the elders and the four living creatures, and they fell on their faces before the throne and worshiped God, 12 saying, "Amen! Blessing and glory and wisdom and thanksgiving and honor and power and might be to our God forever and ever! Amen. (Revelation 7:9-12, ESV)

I don't fully understand all that is portrayed in Revelation 7, but I do see at least one thing very clearly in that passage. When John looks at a multitude of assembled believers that are in Heaven standing before God's throne, he notes that *they are all dressed the same*, but they do not **all LOOK the same**. Somehow, it is evident, that this multitude around the throne comes from all nations, tribes, languages and peoples. Does this mean that humans will somehow maintain their ethnicity in Heaven? Perhaps so, at least in part, because John is able to look at this vast multitude, all dressed alike, and realize immediately that they are incredibly diverse in their appearance, nationality and language.

Consider this: The Heavenly gathering of the Body of Christ is every nation, tribe, language and people, gathered on level ground around the cross, and in front of the Lamb. What a beautiful picture, but is this something that we merely have to look forward to? NO! This is a reality that we are called to cultivate on the earth, and earnestly pray for. Remember that Jesus taught us to pray for the Father's will to be done ON EARTH AS IT IS IN HEAVEN! I take that to mean, in part, that the Body of Christ on earth should reflect the Body of Christ in Heaven. If the Body of Christ on earth is separated by race, economic class, skin color, music preference, dress preference, etc, then we are NOT reflecting the Heavenly reality...and we must.

In 1963, Western Michigan University President Dr. James Miller asked Martin Luther King Jr. a question about segregation, and about whether desegregation should start in churches or schools. Dr. Miller believed that churches had to lead the way forward – that the only way for desegregation to happen in the schools was for the churches to desegregate first. I find Dr. King's answer compelling, and somewhat tragic, considering that our schools integrated long ago (more properly reflecting a Heavenly reality) and our churches still struggle to reflect Revelation 7. Here's what Dr. King said, in full:

> As a preacher, I would certainly have to agree with this. I must admit I have gone through those moments when I was greatly disappointed with the church and what it has done in this period of social change. We must face the fact in America, the church is still the most segregated major institution. At 11:00 on Sunday morning when we stand and sing, and Christ has no east or west, we stand at the most segregated hour in this nation. This is tragic. Nobody of honesty can overlook this.
>
> Now, I'm sure if the church had taken a stronger stand all along, we wouldn't have many of the problems we have. The first way the church can repent, the first way it can move out into the arena of social reform is to remove the yoke of segregation from its own body. The church, itself, will stand under the judgment of God. Now that the mistake of the past has been made, I think the opportunity of the future is to really go out and to transform American society, and where else is there a better place than in the institution that should serve as the moral guardian of the community, the institution that should preach brotherhood and make it a reality within its own body.

Just three years before Dr. King's famous assertion that the 11 AM hour is the most segregated hour in America, Dr. Bob Jones, a white pastor, and the founder of Bob Jones University, addressed tens of thousands of Americans on EASTER Sunday. He told them that he was about to give them "one of the most important and most timely messages," that he had ever shared. He further urged Americans to stop what they were doing, to move closer to the radio, and to listen intently. What was to be the subject of his message? Surely, on Easter Sunday, it would have to be on the most important event in history, right? Surely, on Easter Sunday, a faithful preacher would proclaim the resurrection of the savior...right? Unfortunately, Dr. Jones' message that day would be a 'scriptural' defense of segregation in churches. Bob Jones University would ultimately transcribe the sermon, print it in books and bulletins, and distribute it worldwide. Below are some selections from what Jones had to share that day. I've reprinted about one third of his sermon – which is a large amount – not because I agree with it, but because I think it is important to understand the mindset that has led to segregated churches in 2017 and beyond.

Note below how Jones uses ONE scriptural principle (that God originally placed people in the boundaries of nations) and uses that principle to build an entire understanding of how the Body of Christ should look and operate, clearly ignoring other Scripture, such as Acts 13, just a few chapters prior to Acts 17. Had Dr. Jones done anything more than give a cursory thought to Acts 13, he would have realized that the church in Antioch – the one that launched the original missionary journeys of Paul and Barnabas, as well as being the first place that followers of Christ were called Christians – was a multi-cultural church in the extreme.

The Antioch church was located in modern day Turkey, and contained some Jewish believers like Paul (born in Tarsus, and a citizen of Rome.), Barnabas, a Jewish believer that was born in Cyprus, an island nation in the Mediterranean), Lucius (who was born in Cyrene, a North-African part of Libya), and Simeon called Niger, which means black. We don't know where Simeon was from, but he was probably an African born Jew, based on his nickname. Further, Acts 11:36 says that the church in Antioch was also made up of "Hellenists," which were Greek speaking non-Jewish people. Therefore, we can know with absolute biblical certainty, that the church of Antioch, a strong, missionary sending church in the first century, was composed of believers from at least 5 different countries, and 3 continents. (Israel, Turkey, Rome, Cyprus, Cyrene, and Africa, Asia and Europe.) Keep this in mind as you read Dr. Jones' address below. Keep in mind also, that the implications of Dr. Jones' segregationist philosophy is that the 'white man,' should have never left the affixed boundaries of their race to come and colonize America.

*Now, we folks at Bob Jones University believe that whatever the Bible says is so, and we believe it says certain fundamental things that all Bible-believing Christians accept; but when the Bible speaks clearly about any subject, that settles it. **Men do not always agree, because some people are dumb**--some people are spiritually dumb; but when the Bible is clear, there is not any reason why everybody should not accept it....In recent years there has been a subtle, Satanic effort to undermine people's faith in the Bible; and the devil has led the race along until men have put their own opinion above the Word of God.*

You will find that practically all the troubles we are having today have come out of the fact that men in many instances have ceased to believe in an authoritative Bible...There is no trouble between a born-again white man and a born-again colored man or a born-again Chinese or a born-again Japanese. Born-again, Bible-believing Christians do not have trouble. They may not understand some things; but when we give them the Word of God for it, they see it and understand it....

[Trouble Comes When Nations Break Out of Bounds of Their Fixed Habitation, Contrary to God's Clear Word]

*Paul said that God ". . . hath made of one blood all nations of men .
. . ." But He also fixed the bounds of their habitation. When nations
break out of their boundaries and begin to do things contrary to
the purpose of God and the directive will of God, they have trouble.
The world is in turmoil today because men and nations go contrary
to the clear teaching of the Word of God.
[Why You Cannot Talk about a Superior Race and an Inferior Race]
You talk about a superior race and an inferior race and all that
kind of situation. Wait a minute. No race is inferior in the will of
God. Get that clear. If a race is in the will of God, it is not inferior.
It is a superior race. You cannot be superior to another race if your
race is in the will of God and the other race is in the will of God.*

*[No Two Races Have Ever Gotten Along So Well as the Whites and
the Coloreds in the South]
For many years we have lived together. Occasionally there will be a
flare-up. But the white people have helped the colored people build
their churches, and we have gotten along together harmoniously
and peacefully; and everything has come along fine. Sometimes
we have a little trouble, but then we adjust everything sensibly and
get back to the established order. But the good white folks have
always stood by their good colored friends, and the good colored
folks have always stood by their good white friends. No two races
ever lived as close together as the white people and the colored
people here in the South and got along so well.
[The Effort Today to Disturb God's Plan and Established Order]
Now, what is the matter? There is an effort today to disturb the
established order. Wait a minute. Listen, I am talking straight to
you. White folks and colored folks, you listen to me. You cannot
run over God's plan and God's established order without having*

trouble. God never meant to have one race. It was not His purpose at all. God has a purpose for each race.

[Outsider Agitators in the Name of Piety]

Individually, Christian people in the South-white and black-through the years have been able to work together and to understand each other. But now a world of outside agitation has been started, and people are coming in the name of piety, but it is a false piety, and are endeavoring to disturb God's established order; and we are having turmoil all over America. This disturbing movement is not of God. It is not in line with the Bible. It is Satanic. Now, listen and understand this. Do not let people lead you astray.

[This Agitation Is Satanic Propaganda]

I want you folks to listen-you white and you colored folks. Do not let these Satanic propagandists fool you. This agitation is not of God. It is of the devil. Do not let people slander God Almighty. God made it plain. God meant for Christian people to treat each other right. If you are a Christian white person or a Christian colored person, you will treat each other right. We Christians are children of God by faith in Jesus Christ. We are one in Christ; but let us remember that the God Who made of one blood all nations also fixed the boundaries of their habitations.

Wherever we have the races mixed up in large numbers, we have trouble. They have trouble in New York. They have trouble in San Francisco. They have had trouble all over California. Back in the old days when I was a young fellow, Captain Richmond Pearson Hobson went up and down this country and lectured on the "yellow peril" and told us we were owing to have trouble with Japan. He said there would be a war with Japan some day. People said, "Oh, well, he is crazy." Other leaders went over this country and lectured on the "yellow peril" and the dangers we were facing. Remember, we did have a war with Japan...

If we would just listen to the Word of God and not try to overthrow God's established order, we would not have any trouble. God never meant for America to be a melting pot to rub out the line between the nations. That was not God's purpose for this nation. When someone goes to overthrowing His established order and goes around preaching pious sermons about it, that makes me sick–for a man to stand up and preach pious sermons in this country and talk about rubbing out the line between the races–I say it makes me sick.

God put the Africans over there. They are fine people. They are intelligent people. Do not think they are inferior in every way. It is not so. But we should have sent missionaries over there, and Africa should have been a great nation of colored Christians. If we had done what God had told us to do and sent the Gospel to them and made a Christian nation out of them instead of bringing them over here and selling them into slavery, Africa could have been a great nation of colored Christians. What we did was wrong. It was not right. It cannot be justified. We should not try to justify it. But people went along. Some good people fell for it and went ahead with it; and God overruled it.

I will venture there is not a population in the world where there is a larger percentage of professing Christians than among the colored people in the South. We Christian white people all have good friends among the colored people. The colored Christian people are sensing the dangers we are facing now. There is already an uprising among good, Christian colored people in the South. They are trying to fight back the subtle, Satanic disturbance we have in this country.

[White Southerners Have Never Been More Eager to Help the Colored]

There has never been a time, especially in the last ten years, when the white people in the South were so eager to help the colored people build their schools and see that they get what they ought to have. All this agitation going on is not headed up by real, Bible–believing, Christian people.

[Religious Liberals Are the Worst Infidels]
These religious liberals are the worst infidels in many ways in the
country; and some of them are filling pulpits down South. They
do not believe the Bible any longer; so it does not do any good to
quote it to them. They have gone over to modernism, and they
are leading the white people astray at the same time; and they
are leading colored Christians astray. But every good, substantial,
Bible-believing, intelligent, orthodox Christian can read the Word
of God and know that what is happening in the South now is not
of God.

[If You Are Against Racial Separation, You Are Against Almighty
God]
Yes, God chose the Jews. If you are against segregation and against
racial separation, then you are against God Almighty because He
made racial separation in order to preserve the race through whom
He could send the Messiah and through whom He could send the
Bible. God is the author of segregation. God is the author of Jewish
separation and Gentile separation and Japanese separation. God
made of one blood all nations, but He also drew the boundary lines
between races.

[Colored People Should Remember All That White People Have
Done for Them]
After the Civil War the colored people wanted to build their schools
and churches, and white friends made financial contribution to
the building of these schools and churches. Back in those days
it was not easy when the white folks were paying most of the
taxes-don't you colored friends forget that when you are inclined
to turn away from your white friends. You colored people might
also remember that your ancestry in the South who were slaves
breathed an atmosphere of culture back in those pre-Civil War
days. Think of what your ancestors received in such an atmosphere.
Think of the religion that they learned and how they found God in
slavery days. Think of those old white preachers who preached to

your colored ancestors when they were slaves.

Now listen, the time has come when we ought to sit down and go to thinking some things through in this country. And you colored people listening to me and you white people listening to me ought to keep your heads cool and your minds clear and your hearts warm and keep up these friendly relations we have had through the years. Do not let this outside, Communistic, Hellish influence disturb the friendly relation we have had in the South....

But racially we have separation in the Bible. Let's get that clear. Any race has a right to come to America. We do not mean that when we came over here we wiped out the line between races. We did not do that. We should have let the Africans stay in Africa instead of bringing them here for slaves, but did you colored people ever stop to think where you might have been if that had not happened? Now, you colored people listen to me. If you had not been brought over here and if your grandparents in slavery days had not heard that great preaching you might not even be a Christian. You might be over there in the jungles of Africa today, unsaved. But you are here in America where you have your own schools and your own churches and your own liberties and your own rights, with certain restrictions that God Almighty put about you–restrictions that are in line with the Word of God. The Jews have lived a separated race. They have been separated from the other races of the world. They have been miraculously preserved. Now they have a homeland. They are back there today, and what a wonderful thing is happening...

[Keep Your Bible Where It Belongs]

Now, I am appealing to you colored people and to you white people. Let's use our heads. Let's be intelligent. Let's not try to kick the Bible off the center table. Keep your Bible where it belongs. When they tell you that God Almighty is not the author of the boundaries of nations, you tell them that is wrong. You tell them it is perfectly clear in the Bible that God made of one blood all nations but that

He also fixed the bounds of their habitation. There is nothing unscriptural about that.

[A Christian Can Have Fellowship with a Christian of Another Race, but Not Enter Marital Union with Another Race]

Now I can sit down with any Christian Japanese, and Christian Chinese, and Christian African, etc., anywhere in the world and as a Christian have fellowships. That is a different relationship. A Christian relationship does not mean a marriage relationship. You can be a Christian and have fellowship with people that you would not marry and that God does not want you to marry and that if you should marry you would be marrying outside the will of God. Why can't you see that? Why can't good, solid, substantial people who do not have any prejudices and do not have any hatred and do not have any bitterness see this? **Let's approach this thing in a Christian way. Let's make the battle a Christian battle.** Do not let people run over you by coming along and talking about the Universal Fatherhood of God and the Universal Brotherhood of man. There is no Universal Fatherhood of God and Universal Brotherhood of man. There is not a word about that in the Bible.

[Rubbing Out the Lines Between the Races Is Preparation for the AntiChrist]

If you are a Christian, you are not going to mistreat anybody. You will not mistreat a colored man or a white man or anybody else. Individually, we are one in Christ; but God has also fixed the boundaries of nations, and these lines cannot be rubbed out without having trouble. The darkest day the world has ever known will be when we have one world like they are talking about now. The line will be rubbed out, and the Antichrist will take over and sit down on the throne and rule the world for a little while; and there will be judgment and the cataclysmic curses found in the book of Revelation. We are going to face all this. May God help us to see it and to be true and faithful to Him.

[A Prayer]

Our heavenly Father, bless our country. We thank Thee for our ancestors. We thank Thee for the good, Christian people–white and black. We thank Thee for the ties that have bound these Christian white people and Christian colored people together through the years, and we thank Thee that white people who had a little more money helped them build their churches and stood by them and when they got sick, they helped them. No nation has ever prospered or been blessed like the colored people in the South. Help these colored Christian not to get swept away by all the propaganda that is being put out now. Help us to see this thing and to understand God's established order and to be one in Christ and to understand that God has fixed the boundaries of the nations so we would not have trouble and misunderstanding. Keep us by Thy power and use us for They glory, for Jesus' sake. Amen. (Bob Jones Sermon from April, 1960. Source: https://blogs.thegospelcoalition.org)

Of this sermon, the words of Lemuel Haynes can well be applied, *"[Satan] is a very successful preacher. He draws a great number after him. No preacher can command hearers like him... He mixes truth with error, in order to make it go well, or to carry his point."*

There are so many scriptural errors in Dr. Jones sermon, that it would take an entirely different book to refute them all. Simply because God affixed national boundaries centuries before Christ does not indicate that races and nationalities cannot mix, marry, nor worship together. If Dr. Jones could have taken off his racist worldview glasses, he could have looked at Scripture and clearly seen multiple examples of multi-cultural churches in Scripture, including the ORIGINAL church in the book of Acts, made up of 3000 people from many nations, according to Acts 2. There is absolutely nothing in Scripture that indicates that God desires His churches to be racially distinct from each other, and volumes of evidence that clearly shows that the church on earth, should be as the people of God in Heaven – every nation, tongue and tribe worshiping before the throne of God and the Lamb.

I am grateful that God raised up men like Billy Graham in the 1960s, a southern-born Southern Baptist who had a far more biblical and powerful message to the country than did Bob Jones Sr. The statement below was release by Billy Graham also during Easter week of 1960, and though it is far shorter than Dr. Jones' 'sermon,' it is also exponentially more important and true.

> *The whole trend of Scriptural teaching is toward racial understand-ing. Many use the Scriptures that were applied to Israel. It is true that God called Israel to be unique among the nations and told them to separate themselves from the evil nations round about them. But the white race cannot possibly claim to be the chosen race nor can the white race take for themselves promises that were applied to ancient Israel. . . . Jim Crow must go. It is absolutely ridiculous to refuse food or a night's lodging to a man on the basis of skin color.*
>
> *Modern communications and travel have made the entire world a neighborhood. Who is our neighbor? Jesus gave us the answer in the parable of the Good Samaritan, and yet the Samaritan showed who his neighbor was by helping a person of another race. . . . The message of Christ has led to many great social revolutions and upheavals in history. We are certainly living in one of those crucial periods of social change at the moment, largely caused by the penetration of the teaching of the Scriptures. These periods of history are not easy nor can this type of social change take place over night. Great love, understanding and patience must be exercised by all. (Billy Graham, April 1960. Source: Billy Graham Speaks Out on the Segregation Question," St. Petersburg Times 16 April 1960, 29)*

It is a modern tragedy that our churches are still mostly segregated on Sunday mornings. I am the pastor of a church in Birmingham,

Alabama, and it frequently concerns me that our church is mostly white. Yes, we have several African-American and Hispanic families that regularly worship with us, but our church does not fully reflect our surrounding community, and it certainly doesn't reflect the heavenly reality of Revelation 7. The next chapter will offer some concrete AND spiritual action steps which will war against church segregation and pave the way for unity, and I believe those steps are necessary and helpful.

Those suggestions will not be substitutes, however, for the fullness of what is needed in order to dismantle church segregation in the Western world. I am planning an upcoming book to discuss that issue - how to break down the racial walls between churches in American...but, if I can be completely transparent...I do not yet have good answers, and I have not yet read anybody that does. I plan on spending time with pastors and church leaders of other tribes, nations and languages over the next few months, and prayerfully seeking answers with them. I expect that our black, Hispanic, and other brothers will have wisdom on this issue that far exceeds my own.

Lord, let your church on earth look and operate as it is in Heaven!

12

A Way Forward

Earlier in the book I quoted Nebraska Senator Ben Sasse, who suggested that, after several months of racial upheaval in America, we might be headed for violence. I agree that violence is a possibility.

I do not believe that it is inevitable, however. The people of Jesus are called to be salt and light in this world, and this is as opportune a time to walk in that calling as there has ever been. Consider these words of the only real Master that there is:

> You are the salt of the earth. But if the salt should lose its taste, how can it be made salty? It's no longer good for anything but to be thrown out and trampled on by men. 14 "You are the light of the world. A city situated on a hill cannot be hidden. 15 No one lights a lamp and puts it under a basket, but rather on a lampstand, and it gives light for all who are in the house. 16 In the same way, let your light shine before men, so that they may see your good works and give glory to your Father in heaven. (Matthew 5:13-16)

This is a right now command of Jesus to His church to intervene and be savory salt and bright light. I believe that it is possible, if Christians would prayerfully begin to radiate the truth of the gospel and the love of Jesus, that we could avert more race-based violence in the western world. Not ALL of it, certainly, but much of it. Lest you think I am being a naive Pollyanna, let me suggest seven ways in which the church can practically, effectively, fruitfully, and boldly meet the challenge of racial strife right now. (Note: this chapter is, of necessity, quite short. It is hoped that it will represent a bridge to a follow-up work on race and racism that will explore potential paths forward in more than just a cursory manner.)

1. Search for and repent of personal racism. Most people reading this now will think for a moment, and quickly conclude that they are not racists. Bob Jones, Sr. didn't think he was a racist either, and loudly proclaimed the equality of all races, and yet he continued to lead people down the road of racist segregation throughout his life.

Multiple passages in the Bible call followers of God to self-examination in a way similar to Lamentations 3:40, "**Let us test and** *examine our ways, and return to the Lord!*" It is good for Christians of all races to ponder our own ways. What are the subtle (and obvious!) ways that we are contributing to racism? I read Dr. Jones' sermon in the previous chapter, and shake my head, wondering how in the world that he didn't identify and repent of much of the unbiblical racist sewage that he was sharing. It jars me to think that similar thoughts and ideals could be in me, but chances are, they probably are! I like how Scott Clark on the Heidelblog walks his readers through the issue of racism:

> *Even under the traditional definition [of racism] we must admit that there is racism in our hearts and in our midst. If we deny it then we are deluding ourselves and denying our own doctrine. In The Heidelberg Confession 5 we confess that we are prone by nature to hate God and our neighbor. Racism is among those sins against which we must fight all our lives . In Heidelberg 60 we confess that even though we are justified by grace alone through faith alone, nevertheless, even in a state of grace, "I have grievously sinned against all the commandments of God, and have never kept any of them, and am still prone always to all evil...". We are not perfectionists...*
>
> *What to do? The first thing to do is to recognize that this is not a new sin. The Apostle Paul had been a racist. As a Pharisee of Pharisees he despised "Gentile dogs" (Phil 3:2) as inferior simply because they were not Jewish. There were Jewish Christians who were still disgusted by Greek and Roman converts.*
>
> *Second, because racism is an ancient sin and because it is addressed by Scripture, we need to think about it in biblical and confessional categories. We should not make it a special sin nor the unforgivable sin. Second, we should expose it and address it openly.*
>
> *We need to be realistic about the depth and width of the sin of racism in our hearts and in our churches. It will remain a struggle, but if we admit that we are sinners, if we do not pretend to have*

arrived or to have been perfected (Phil 3:12) then we can admit what we are: simultaneously justified and sinner (simul iustus et peccator).

If we are not pretending to have arrived, then we can and must hear admonition from our brothers and sisters. If our congregations are marked by an openness about the pervasive reality of sin as well as the transforming reality of grace, we can and will become welcoming congregations where all the nations are gathered together at the feet of Jesus worshiping and serving together and reflecting the inaugurated (but not yet consummated) final reality of the new heavens and the new earth. (Source: heidelblog.net/2017/08/
houston-we-do-have-a-problem

2. Work towards corporate racism repentance. When I suggest that the way forward includes working towards corporate racism repentance, I am specifically targeting the 'corporate' church, with corporate indicating the Body of Christ in its togetherness, not as individuals. I am specifically using the verb "work" here, because I believe that this step involves actions more than mere talking, posting and writing.

It is the easiest thing in the world to criticize other people. Social media and the internet have made it easier than ever to do so. As I type this, there are tens of thousands of people on social media right now lambasting Houston pastor Joel Osteen for not opening 'his' church in Houston for Hurricane Harvey victims. The vast majority of those people (with a few exceptions) have not lifted a finger to help hurricane victims, they just want to take a shot at Osteen. I am not a fan of Joel Osteen at all, but I think the vast majority of criticisms I have read in this instance have been quite unfair, considering that they were coming from people who were *also not helping*, and considering that the church apparently received a massive load of beds one day after the storm in preparation to actually be a hurricane shelter.

I mention the criticisms of Osteen to make one clear point: I don't believe the way forward is criticism and attacking other people on the issue of race. Jesus taught us to worry about the plank in our own eye before we go after the splinter in other's eyes. You are NOT helping racial unity in America when your 'ministry' is simply criticizing unenlightened, barbarian Christians for being racist. The fact is that there are already PLENTY of professional critics writing these days. Neither the church nor the nation needs another voice of criticism and condemnation...instead, WORK <u>towards</u> racial unity, and WORK <u>away</u> from corporate racism. Have conversations with people. Study the Word of God together and consider well the call of Jesus to 'oneness.' Do everything in your power to move towards racial unity in the name of Jesus.

Here is at least one concrete way of doing this. Jarvis Williams and Kevin Jones' recent book, *Removing the Stain of Racism from the Southern Baptist Convention*, notes that it is rare in Southern Baptist seminaries to read books by or about persons of color. As I have pondered my seminary experience (6 years of taking seminary classes and another 9 years of actually working for a seminary), I realize that Williams and Jones are absolutely right – There are few textbooks that are used by authors of another color, and few illustrations, anecdotes and teaching in regards to famous preachers and church leaders of other colors and nationalities. How can we overcome this problem? Well, for starters, teachers can include books and resources from Godly black, Hispanic, Asian and other languages and nationalities. Jones and William's book would be an excellent start in that direction!

3. Be quick to listen, slow to speak, and slow to become angry. During the Charlottesville race controversy of August, 2017, I noted that most people – including most Christians – were very slow to listen and understand, quick to speak, and extremely swift to become angry, almost as if they had access to the anger version of the Speed Force. Christians should NOT be like that. They should be slow to

react to some things, because they are practicing the admonition of James 1:19, and listening well rather than speaking with anger quickly. I think if James were writing today, he would also say, "Be slow to post angrily."

Consider the current kerfuffle about Confederate statues. I have seen many of my (mostly white) Christian friends loudly and vehemently contend against the removal of Confederate statues, advocating for their preservation on historical, or other grounds. I get that sentiment, and understand it. I am a Civil War buff, and a collegiate history teacher. The Civil War was complicated, and there is much we can learn from it. I'm not sure that the best way to handle the Civil War is to just put away all of the statues. I wonder, however, if those who are advocating for the preservation of historical Confederate statues have considered things from a black perspective.

I can completely see why black Christians, or northern Christians, or other reasonable people could have problems with those statues – especially the ones that venerate their subjects as great people, and are proudly displayed by cities in their public squares. Go back to chapter 8 and reread some of the rhetoric of the pro-slavery pastors, and how they dehumanized black people. While it is true that not everybody in the Confederacy had those views, it is equally true that many of them did, including some (most?) of the prominent leaders of the day. If I was black, it would infuriate me to honor some of those Confederate men, and it would bother me to see those statues placed in the most prominent areas of many Southern towns. When it comes to complicated issues such as this, I am suggesting that it is unbiblical, even foolish, to proclaim our views loudly and proudly (and quickly!) on social media. Wisdom and the Bible require us to be slow to speak. Yes – we might miss out on some hot takes, and quick reactions, but Christians aren't supposed to be the 'hot take' people.

4. Seek peace and pursue it. Both Psalm 34 and 1 Peter 3 advocate the active pursuit of peace:

"Whoever desires to love life and see good days,
let him keep his tongue from evil and his lips from speaking deceit;
11 let him turn away from evil and do good; let him seek peace
and pursue it. 12 For the eyes of the Lord are on the righteous,
and his ears are open to their prayer. But the face of the Lord is
against those who do evil." (1 Peter 3:10-12)

Jesus called His followers to be peaceMAKERS. Romans 14 commands the PURSUIT of peace. Hebrews 12:14 urges believers to STRIVE for peace with everyone. Peace is not portrayed in Scripture as the result of simply not causing conflict. Peace is something that must be made, pursued, striven after, and found. Applying this principle to the issue of race demonstrates that racial unity, and the oneness that Jesus prayed for, will not come about by simply not being racist. Peace between races must be pursued. Pursuit calls for intentionality – we need to intentionally pursue other nations, ethnic groups and tribes for relationship and partnership. This won't be easy, and misunderstandings must be expected, but if the goal remains peace, unity and the oneness that Jesus prayed for, those misunderstandings don't have to be barriers, but mere speed-bumps.

5. Avoid virtue-signalling. I believe that the concepts of "virtue-signalling," "privilege," and "trigger-alerts," will not be nearly as prominent in ten years as they are currently. Nevertheless, virtue-signalling is a thing now, and it should be avoided as much as possible in pursuing biblical racial harmony. What, exactly, is virtue-signalling? According to Dictionary.com, it is:

"The action or practice of publicly expressing opinions or senti-
ments intended to demonstrate one's good character or the moral
correctness of one's position on a particular issue. Often virtue
signaling consists of saying you hate things"

Most people are guilty of virtue-signalling, I know I am. For the most part, however, it is not very helpful. It takes wisdom to know when to speak up about a particular issue, and when to be silent. When the prime motivation for speaking on a particular issue, especially a race issue, is to make yourself appear virtuous and wise, that is the time to keep quiet.

6. Cultivate Diversity. Did you shudder a little bit when you read that sentence? I did when I wrote it, because it sounds so much like a buzz-word laden corporate slogan that has no real meaning. However, if we desire to pursue the oneness that Jesus prayed for, and for the church on earth to be as the saints are in Heaven, we will need to pursue cultural diversity in our churches. Neither all white church staffs, nor all black church staffs will produce a Revelation 7 church. Whitewashed seminary curriculum (the kind that mostly ignores Christians from other tribes, languages and ethnic groups) will not produce a Revelation 7 church. And sitting around bemoaning your lack of friends and brothers/sisters in Christ that are of another color will not suddenly cause you to befriend somebody. If we are serious about racial harmony, then we should seek to cultivate it in our family relationships, on our church staffs, and in our worship gatherings.

7. Listen and Read the Orthodox Biblical Teachings of Different Tribes, Cultures and Ethnicities. I'm not exactly talking about affirmative action theology here, but I am suggesting that history has shown that there are a great number of blind spots in 'white' theology, 'American' theology, 'British' theology, etc. We need to hear from the global Body of Christ, keeping in mind that Paul was a Roman, St. Augustine was an African (and likely black), St. Athanasius was also African and black, and Abraham was from Iraq. Here is a good list of faithful and biblical writers/preachers that are a different color than my own, and in no particular order:

1. Thabiti Anyabwile – A black pastor, formerly of the Islamic faith, that was graciously saved by Jesus and now pastors a church in Washington, DC. Thabiti has written *Finding Faithful Elders and Deacons* (with 9 Marks ministries) and *What is a Healthy Church Member?*

2. Voddie Baucham – Voddie is the Dean of African Christian University in Zambia, and a former United States pastor. He has written several important books on family ministry, biblical manhood and womanhood, and other topics.

3. Pastor Juan Sanchez – Juan is the author of *1 Peter For You* (part of an excellent series on the books of the Bible), and is also the pastor of HighPointe church in Austin, Texas.

4. Conrad Mbewe – When your nickname is "The African Spurgeon," that says an awful lot. Mbewe is a pastor and writer in Lusaka, Zambia. He is also a prolific writer, authoring two columns a week for his country's daily newspaper, and also several notable books. Two of his books, *Pastoral Preaching: Building a People for God* and *Prosperity: Seeking the True Gospel* (with Wayne Grudem) are particularly worth your time to read.

4. Eric C. Redmond – A member of the Gospel Coalition, and the author of *Exalting Jesus in Jonah, Micah, Nahum and Habbakuk*, Eric is a pastor and Bible Professor at Moody Bible Institute.

5. H.B. Charles – The Pastor of Shiloh Metropolitan Baptist church in Jacksonville, and the author of an excellent book on preaching, Charles is one of the best preachers in America, and a powerful voice for biblical truth.

6. Afshin Ziafat – Born into an Islamic-American family in Houston, Ziafat lived for a few years with his family in Iran, before returning to

the U.S. and converting to Christianity. He is the co-author of several Gospel Project books (with Matt Chandler) and pastors Providence Church in Frisco, Texas.

7. Kwame Bediako – A theologian and writer from Ghana, Bediako was a Presbyterian who developed an African school theology that was very different from Black Liberation theology, and used Early Church Fathers Clement of Alexandria and Justin Martyr as a model.

8. Jarvis J. Williams – Dr. Williams is a theology professor at The Southern Baptist Theological Seminary in Louisville. He is also the author of the excellent book, *Removing the Stain of Racism from the Southern Baptist Convention.*

9. Dwight McKissic – Pastor and writer McKissic is from Arkansas, and currently pastors in Texas at Cornerstone Baptist Church. He is a prominent voice among Southern Baptists, and is the author of *When Heaven and Earth Collide: Racism, Southern Evangelicals, and the Better Way of Jesus.*

10. Ajith Fernando – Ajith is a Sri Lankan theologian and evangelist, and leads the Youth For Christ effort in his home country. Ajith has suffered well for the Gospel, and has shown amazing character in pointing people to Jesus. He is the author of *Reclaiming Friendship* and *Crucial Questions about Hell.* As I write this, I am quite ashamed, because I am realizing that don't know nearly enough Asian or Hispanic theologians and writers. I've actually reached out to some friends on social media to help rectify this situation.

11. Dr. David Eung-Yul Ryoo – Dr. Ryoo is a past professor at Chongshin Theological Seminary in South Korea, and is currently pastoring the Korean Central Presbyterian church in Centreville, Virginia. As mentioned in chapter 2, Dr. Ryoo is an expert on the

Moravian missions model, and his church is extremely active in the Washington, DC. area, particularly among the large Korean population there.

Shoutout to the Reformed Pub, on Facebook, who helped me to compile this list, which is very incomplete, but represents a good beginning. Thanks in particular to Ryan Burton King (who introduced me to Dr. Ryoo), Jasmine Holmes, daughter of Voddie Baucham (who recommended Conrad Mbewe for this list, and added, quite jokingly, that her father was a bit 'overrated.'), Stuart Chase, Red Baron Broadway, Todd Seay, Thomas Mikoski, Jordan Chase, Ryan Matthew, Cristian Rogers, Louis Lyons, Adam Young, Priscilla Henry, Jay Lloyd, Brad Jones, and Ileana Forment. I intend to expand this list significantly in the coming months, and post it to my website, www.Chaseathompson.com/blog

13

The Puritans: Good Theology + Racism?

Thabiti Anyabwile preaching.

Good theology does not mechanically lead to good living. We need to understand this. It's a commonplace Christian assertion that if we believe the right things we ought to do the right things. Then we're perplexed when either people who believe the right things actually do vile things, or people with supposedly faulty theology actually live better than the orthodox. We're left groping for explanations and defenses. How did the Puritans "miss it"? Why did "liberals" seem to "get it"? Well, "it" doesn't follow mechanically, ipso facto, ex opere operato from some set of solid beliefs. There's a whole lot of effort, application, resistance to the world, self-examination, and mortification that's gotta accompany the doctrine in order for the duty to follow. As Flav put it, "They're blind, baby, because they can't see." That's why they missed it; they couldn't see it.

*Their theology wasn't a corrective lens; it didn't fix the cataracts. It didn't fix the degenerative sight of Southern Presbyterians who also missed it, or the Dutch Reformed of South Africa who not only missed it but supported Apartheid, or some of the German Reformed who missed it in Nazi Germany, and so on. And this is why I'm made slightly nervous by the tendency of some Reformed types to advocate "pure" doctrine and demur at "pure" social action. The Puritan movement was a movement in church reform and revival, and some of their heirs (I count myself one) can be too purely concerned about the purity of the church without a commen-surate concern about the purity of social witness. **We can stack our chips on theology, as though theology inexorably produces the social results we want with little to no attending effort. Mistake, I think. The Puritans prove that.** (Thabiti Anyabwile – Source: https://blogs.thegospelcoalition.org/thabitianyabwile/*

The above excerpt, from an article by Gospel Coalition writer Thabiti Anyabwile, wrestles with the fact that, though the Puritans had good theology (in many ways), many of them still owned and mistreated slaves. Thabiti's point is that pursuing sound theology alone is not enough. Sound theology must be combined with active, biblical love. 1st John 3:18 demonstrates how this works: "**Little children, we must not love with word or speech, but with truth and action. This is how we** *will know we belong to the truth and will convince our conscience in His presence."* Belonging to the truth and being a people of love is never simply a matter of having right beliefs, but it is always about having right beliefs that produce action and fruit.

To solidify Thabiti's perspective on the Puritans and, far more importantly, to learn how to avoid their errors, let us consider a few excerpts from the treatise *Domestical Duties* by Puritan pastor William Gouge as a sort of exemplar for Puritan thoughts on slavery. This book, which has almost 700 pages, was written by Pastor Gouge for his people in Blackfriars, London, and gives volumes of practical instruction on marriage, business, child-raising, being a servant, and being a master. The selections below are from treatise 7, and give highly specific directions as to what a master should do and should not do. (There are several pages of instructions given on when to beat servants, and when not to, and how far is too far in terms of administering beatings. Reading just a couple of those pages is more than enough to see the point that Thabiti is making.) Note: the text in brackets below is my own, and the text has been slightly modernized.

> *Masters [must] keep their servants in awe and fear. [Since] Children must be kept in subjection: how much more servants....*
>
> *1. Masters ought not to be so forward as to strike servants that are grown in years, as they would strike the younger sort. Years bring understanding, and a rebuke will make one of understanding more sorry for a fault, and more careful to amend it, The direction prescribed to parents (from an earlier part of this book.) for well ordering that correction which they give to their children, may in many points be here fitly applied. Read it.*
>
> *Then blows: {a} hard blow works more upon the younger sort. But if notwithstanding their years they be stubborn, and will not listen to your words, their stubborness must be beaten down with blows. Smite a scorner, saith the wise man: and again, judgments are prepared for scorners, and stripes for the back of fools.*

Seeing older servants are in this case to be corrected, it is further requisite to put a difference between the kind or measure of correction which is given to them, and to the younger sort: if they are corrected as children, they may either make a toy of it, or the more disdain at it. blessedness, wound, and stripes piercing into the inward parts of the belly, are a purging medicine against evil, to stubborn servants of ripe years. [I am not 100 percent sure what Gouge is conveying here.]

2. If there be a master and mistress who are joint governors over an house, it is fittest for the master to correct men-servants and the mistress maids. Abraham put his maid over to Sarah in such a case. Yet if a maid should grow stubborn, and mannish, and turn against her mistress, she being weak, sickly, with child, or otherwise unable to master her maid, the master may and must beat down her stubbornness and rebellion: so much did the law of God permit. (Domestical Duties, p. 654)

Notice how Gouge clearly links the duties of a master to discipline servants with the duties of a father to discipline children, a link that the Bible nowhere makes or implies. Also, In the above sentences, Gouge prescribes heavier beatings for younger servants and lighter beatings for older servants, unless they persist in their stubbornness, in which case they are to also be beaten with heavy blows. While Gouge does elsewhere say that masters can't beat their servants out of anger, and they can't beat their servants to death or lameness, the above is still plenty offensive, in particular the parts about a male master having a duty before God to beat down stubborn and strong female servants.

See also how Gouge quotes Scripture to justify his counsel – in particular Old Testament Scripture. He uses the case of Abraham's actions in the Hagar matter as a model for behavior. It should be pointed out that the Abraham/Sarah/Hagar affair is portrayed in a very negative light in Genesis, and it gives warrant to the mistreatment of slaves no more than 1st Samuel gives warrant to those who might want to have the husband of a beautiful bathing maid killed, in order to marry her.

Some of the actions of the characters in the Old Testament are blatantly wrong, and not to be copied, but Gouge her builds theology and practical instruction on these narrative stories (rather than clear teachings) and ends up giving monstrous advice because of it. In some of Gouge's other words, one can see more hopeful statements, the kind of statements that would sow the seeds of Puritan Richard Baxter's later call for abolition, and would ultimately lead to Puritans like Samuel Sewall and Jonathan Edwards, Jr. becoming vocal supporters of abolition and condemners of race-based slavery. An example of that can be seen here in his rules for giving servants rest (though 5-7 hours was probably not nearly enough sleep!)

> Intermission, ease, and rest from labor at seasonable times, is as needful and requisite, as food and apparel. The reason which God renders of the fourth commandment shows that masters ought to afford rest to their servants: it is this, that thy servant may rest. Without intermission and rest the body cannot endure labor: it will wax weak, faint, and utterly unable to continue: but, as labor decays strength, so rest repairs it. There are two especial times of rest, which servants may not be denied. 1. The rest of the night. 2. The rest of the Lords day. Question: What time may be thought sufficient to afford sleep unto servants? Answer: As the same quantity of food is not over-strictly to be proportioned to all alike, so nor the same continuance of sleep. Yet by experience it hath been observed that for sound and healthy bodies, five hours is the least time that may be allowed, and seven hours is time sufficient for any.(Domestical Duties, 675)

Even more importantly, read below to see how Gouge made the unmistakable case (over and against Confederate preachers and slave-owners) that slaves and masters were fully equal in the sight of God

God will do the same things to all sorts of masters that they do to their servants. To the consideration of this impartial Justice of God doth the Apostle call masters, both because of that outward power which they have over their servants, and also because for the most part masters are backed with the power and authority of magistrates on earth, who in matters of difference betwixt master and servant are ordinarily partial, respecting masters more then servants.

But let masters here learn to cast off all such fond conceits, and foolish hopes. Though they be higher in place, have more wealth, and better friends then their servants, and though men who have carnal eyes may thereby be much moved to respect them, yet will not God move a hairs breadth from justice for the whole world. "If the greatest man that ever was in the world should have a servant that were the [lowest in rank] that ever was, and a case betwixt that master and that servant should come before God, God would not any whit at all lean to that master more than to the servant" (Domestical Duties, p. 693)

I suspect (and hope) that nobody reading this will agree with how Gouge's Puritan brethren dealt with African slaves, but on the above point – that all are equal in the site of God and His judgments – the Puritans were spot on. Reading through Gouge's book (and the works of other Puritans who supported slavery), one is struck by several haunting questions. How could he, on the one hand advocate the beating of slaves for punishment (even female slaves!) and, on the other hand, write a line like this, *"God will do the same things to all sorts of masters that they do to their servants."* I think Gouge is spot on with that observation, but I don't understand how he couldn't see more clearly the implications of the truth he was writing about. It seems to me a very strange inconsistency in thought AND in biblical interpretation to convincingly proclaim the equality of all races and classes, while involuntarily enslaving some of them, and doling out physical violence to them. It reeks of hypocrisy in a very deep way, and I am dumbfounded that the Puritans could not see their hypocrisy.

But pounding on the Puritans is not the purpose of this chapter. I am more than disquieted by what they did, and how poorly many of them treated slaves, but they are gone now, and I am not their judge. They will face Him, however, and I am sure Gouge's prediction will come true, and there will be dire consequences for their actions. No, judging is not the purpose of this chapter, but rather it is to call us all to examine our own ways, our own theology, and our own walking out of that theology. The slave-holding and slavery-advocating Puritans were (willfully?) blind in their application of Scripture.

Where are we doing the same thing? What areas of the commands of God are we overlooking in our lives and in the Body of Christ? I am not fully qualified to answer that question, but I would be bold enough to suggest that there are at least three areas where the western church might be tragically overlooking Scripture in a similar manner as did the Puritans.

#1 – The teachings of the Bible on wealth, specifically passages like James 1:10-11, James 2, James 5:1-3, 1 Timothy 6, Luke 6:24, Mark 10:23-25, and Revelation 3:17. The Bible takes a dim view of the pursuit of wealth, and most people who are wealthy have actively pursued it at some point. The church in America – particularly wealthy and prosperous churches – would do well to grapple with the passages mentioned above.

#2 The warnings of the Bible about worldliness. Again, the church in the west is regularly wooed by the things of the World – the TV shows, the sports, the movies, etc. It is extremely difficult to know where to draw the line, but too often, we in the western church tend to minimize the stinging power of passages like 1 John 2:15 ("**Do not love** *the world or the things that belong to the world. If anyone loves the world,* *love for the Father is not in him.*"), 2 Peter 1:4, James 4:4-7, James 1:27, Colossians 2:20, etc.

#3 Our lack of active, sacrificial pursuit of the kind of oneness and unity in the Body of Christ that Jesus prayed for in John 17. We Christians can be a contentious people – leaving churches over small matters and differences of opinion. Creating new denominations over matters of Scripture that aren't worthy of dividing over. Creating whole ministries focused on attacking other Christian leaders. To be clear, not every division is wrong. There is a time to "come out from them and be separate," but far too often Christians in the west take the easier path of separation and division, than the more biblical path of pursuing peace. We should consider well Paul's caution in 1 Corinthians 3:

> Brothers, I was not able to speak to you as spiritual people but as people of the flesh, as babies in Christ. 2 I gave you milk to drink, not solid food, because you were not yet ready for it. In fact, you are still not ready, 3 because you are still fleshly. For since there is envy and strife among you, are you not fleshly and living like unbelievers? 4 For whenever someone says, "I'm with Paul," and another, "I'm with Apollos," are you not unspiritual people? 5 What then is Apollos? And what is Paul? They are servants through whom you believed, and each has the role the Lord has given...16 Don't you yourselves know that you are God's sanctuary and that the Spirit of God lives in you? 17 If anyone destroys God's sanctuary, God will destroy him; for God's sanctuary is holy, and that is what you are.

Please allow me to close out this chapter with a positive word about the Puritans, because I believe that God ultimately used them to set the stage for the eventual dismantling of slavery. They mustn't be praised for how most of them handled issues of race and slavery, but rather denounced for that. However, we can rightly thank God that their biblical belief in the equality of all flesh ultimately had a great impact on the abolitionist movement of the 18th and 19th centuries. Joel Beeke, the scholar par excellence of the Puritans, offers this hopeful end to his essay on the Puritans and slavery:

> Puritan theology contained seeds that slowly grew and blossomed into anti-slavery teachings. Not only did they recognize the humanity of all peoples and our duty to show them love and justice, but they also saw that stealing people to place them in bondage—the fountain and source of slavery—is contrary to biblical ethics. At the end of the sixteenth century, William Perkins, often called the father of Puritanism due to his pervasive influence, said that the Eighth Commandment forbids us "to steal other men's servants, or children" (Golden Chaine [London: John Legat, 1600], 91).
>
> "Man-stealing" (cf. Ex. 21:16; 1 Tim. 1:10) was denounced as a sin by the Puritans in the Westminster Larger Catechism (Q. 142) in the mid-seventeenth century. This became a key term in the Christian polemic against slavery. Richard Baxter, one of the best known Puritans, applied this principle directly to the enslavement of Africans: "To go as pirates and catch up poor negroes or people of another land, that never forfeited life or liberty, and to make them slaves, and sell them, is one of the worst kinds of thievery in the world; and such persons are to be taken for the common enemies of mankind; and they that buy them and use them as beasts, for their mere commodity, and betray, or destroy, or neglect their souls, are fitter to be called incarnate devils than Christians, though they be no Christians whom they so abuse" (Christian Directory [Ligonier, Penn.: Soli Deo Gloria, 1990], 1:462).

By 1700 the Puritan Samuel Sewall was agitating against slavery in The Selling of Joseph. ...In New York, the Scottish minister Alexander McCleod invoked Exodus 21:16 in "Negro Slavery Unjustified" (1802) to lead the Reformed Presbyterians to condemn slavery as **"treason against heaven."** *McCleod did not live in the Puritan era, but he operated under the same theology that characterized the Puritan movement.*

In hindsight we groan over the many years that black slaves had to wait before Christians woke up to a consistent application of their theological principles. Our nation continues to suffer the tragic consequences of this blindness. But we must not reject the theology of the Puritans or the Puritans themselves for their slowness and tunnel-vision in this matter. In every age and culture, true Christians have blindspots such that they tolerate or even promote sins which they should abominate and combat. Our own age no doubt has many. Rather than turning aside from the Puritans, we should recognize their faults but continue to study and learn from them. (Joel Beeke, in "Seeds of Anti-Slavery in Reformed Doctrine." Source www.joelbeeke.org/)

14

16 Christian Passages on the Evils of Racism

This chapter will simply be a large collection of excellent thoughts on race from faithful followers of Christ. I might include a brief amount of commentary on a few of the quotes, but they will stand on their own, by and large. The reason for including all of these quotes is to #1 spur you on towards Godly and Biblical thinking about race and #2 to demonstrate that there have been faithful voices in the worldwide church since the first century that have powerfully and passionately proclaimed good truths about race. Some might think (with reason) that the church in the past has been too often racist. While it is true (and inexcusable) that there have always been racists in every period of church history, I believe it is also true that those Christians who have known, proclaimed and lived biblical truths about race have always outnumbered those who haven't.

> 1. *Sometimes we get a gem amongst the news, and to my mind there was a gem contained in a Reuter's telegram, from Rio Janeiro, May 10th:—"The Brazilian Chamber of Deputies has voted the immediate and unconditional abolition of slavery in Brazil." My heart rejoiced as I read that paragraph. I hope it does not mean that this vote can be defeated in some other Chamber, or the abolition be prevented by some other power; but if it means that slavery is to be immediately and unconditionally abolished in Brazil, I call upon you all to thank God, and rejoice in his name. Wherever slavery exists, it is an awful curse; and the abolition of it is an unspeakable blessing. All free men should praise God, and especially those whom Christ has made free, for they are "free indeed. (Source: 1888 Charles Spurgeon sermon, "Freedom at Once and for Ever," in The Metropolitan Tabernacle Pulpit Sermons, vol. 40 (London: Passmore & Alabaster, 1894), 349.)*

I love Charles Spurgeon very deeply, and I especially love the fact that, even though he was a "product of his time," he was not blinded to the Bible's clear anti-racist teachings and their implications. Slavery is indeed an awful curse, and came about through the curse of Genesis 3 in the garden. Some might even say that slavery is man's attempt to remove the burden of God's curse in the garden ("you shall sweat for every drop of food you eat") from himself and put it onto somebody else.

2. If you're reading through the Bible and you get to Joshua 7 — especially if you're a white American, especially if you're Western person — you go "What?" In Joshua 7, a man named Achan, an Israelite — they're coming into the promised land, they are strictly told you were not here for plunder — Achan takes some plunder, a robe, some wealth, takes it for himself, hides it under his tent. He breaks the law. He goes against God's will, goes against the law for the Israelites. When it's discovered, he's not just punished, but his entire family is stoned to death with him. Western people — especially white Americans — say, "Wait a minute, he did it. They didn't do it!"

Now let me just get right off and say this. Most people and most other cultures, most other centuries understand why that happened. If you're a New Yorker and you have some objection to some part of the Bible that you find offensive, I want you to realize it's your cultural location that's causing the offense. Don't you dare think that just because you find that part of the Bible offensive, everybody in the whole world would think the Bible is offensive. That's culturally narrow of you to think that because most people, most places know that we are not just the product of our choices — individual choices. That if you can do something bad, the fact that you can do it, what helped you become the kind of person that can do it, was to a great degree your family.

Your family produced you directly or at least failed to keep you from becoming that, and therefore at least actively or passively, your family participates in your guilt. Most people, most places, Americans — especially white Americans — don't understand that. Most people, most places recognize that because you're not the product of your own individual choices, you are the product of a community. Not only are you the product of a community to a great degree, but that you by even participating in that community are producing other kinds of people with their particular kinds of character to because of your interaction with them. Joshua 7 says that there is corporate responsibility inside a family.

I'll take it up a little higher. In Daniel 9, now we're talking about corporate guilt and responsibility inside a whole race or a culture because Daniel, in Daniel 9, confesses sins — repents for — and says it's his responsibility to repent for sins that his ancestors did that he didn't do it all.

I mean I still hear it, though especially years ago when I lived in the South. I heard white people say, "Yeah, it's a shame what slavery did, but I never owned any slaves so why in the world does anybody think that I as a white person now had any responsibility to that community over there at all? I didn't own slaves." But here is Daniel feeling a responsibility for and repenting for things his ancestors did. Why? Because he knows that the culture that he's part of produced the sins of the past and he's still part of that culture. He senses the responsibility and the Bible senses the responsibility. He senses the connection. (Pastor Tim Keller, 2012 message. Source: http://www.desiringgod.org/)

Tim Keller, if you are not familiar with him, is not a liberal theologian. He is a conservative, biblical, complementarian pastor in the Presbyterian Church of America, which is one of the most theologically conservative denominations out there. You might not agree with the dynamic that Keller is proposing here, but I believe that he has made a very good biblical case for what he is asserting, which is that we are, in part, defined by our culture and responsible for our culture.

3. Posterity is concerned in the actions of their ancestors or predecessors, in families, nations, and most communities of men, as standing in some respect in their stead. And some particular persons may injure, not only a great part of the world contemporary with them, but may injure and undo all future generations of many individuals, families, or larger communities.

So that men who live now, may have an action against those who lived a thousand years ago; or there may be a cause which needs to be decided by the Judge of the world, between some of the present generation, and some who lived a thousand years ago.

Princes who, by rapine and cruelty, ruin nations, are answerable for the poverty, slavery, and misery of the posterity of those nations. So, as to those who broach and establish opinions and principles, which tend to the overthrow of virtue, and propagation of vice, and are contrary to the common rights and privileges of mankind.—Thus, Mahomet (Mohammed) has injured all succeeding posterity, and is answerable, at least in a degree, for the ruin of the virtue of his followers in many respects, and for the rapine, violence, and terrible devastations which his followers have been guilty of toward the nations of the world, and to which they have been instigated by the principles which he taught them. And, whoever they were, who first drew away men from the true religion, and introduced and established idolatry, they have injured all nations that have to this day partaken of the infection.

Jonathan Edwards, The Works of Jonathan Edwards, vol. 2 (Banner of Truth Trust, 1974), 471.

For those that might have struggled with Keller's idea (above) that we can be somehow responsible or involved with the sins that our ancestors have committed, you might be surprised that Keller's understanding comes from Jonathan Edwards, a pastor and writer used mightily of God in the First Great Awakening. Edwards wrote fairly extensively about the evils of slavery and of man-stealing and abuse, but himself owned slaves. His son, however, came to greater understanding of truth, and released all of the Edwards family slaves six years before the American Revolution, and almost 100 years prior to the Emancipation Proclamation.

> 4. *Tell me what you think, but I've come to the conclusion that the Christian Church desperately needs to be discipled regarding "race," racism and justice. I once thought the most significant deficiency in Christian theology (at least in the West) was a deficiency in the theology of suffering. But I think there's more ink used to help people with suffering than there is to help people think of themselves primarily as Christians and radically apply their new identity in Christ to fallen categories like "race" and insidious sins like racism.*
>
> *It's tragic that the country's biggest sin is racism and the Church's biggest omission is racial justice. The tragedy gets compounded when one remembers that some quarters of the Church were once the strongest supporters of this sin. That means we're working our way out of a deficit. The roots of racism are tangled with our faith. And this means we can't assume some neutral stance, being formally against this sin but practically uninvolved. The root keeps creeping. We had better be weeding the garden of our faith and growing one another up into the fullness of Christ with attention to this anti-Christ called "racism."*
>
> *Over and over the question I get from genuine and well-meaning Christians is, "How can I think about...?" Or, "What should I do about...?" Those are discipleship questions that desperately need answering in every local church—assuming we don't want the roots of racism to find any soil in the body of Christ. (Source: Thabiti Anyabwile https://blogs.thegospelcoalition.org/thabitianyabwile)*

Thabiti, as an African-American pastor, writes a lot about race. I used to sort of naively think that it was more important to use all of our energies and ink focusing on Jesus and His gospel over and above anything else. I still believe that to be the case, but the fact is that the good news of Jesus has implications and practical impacts, which means we must write about issues like race and racism, and grapple with how the Word of God calls us to act in regards to them. I absolutely agree with Thabiti that the church has been complicit in racism too often in the past, and it has diminished and damaged our shining of the gospel. We do indeed need biblical discipling in the areas of race, racism, and justice. We need to think about it more, write about it more, pray for racial unity more, and walk out biblical racial justice more and more. I am hopeful that this book represents one very tiny step in that direction.

5. *[You might say] "I got me slaves and slave-girls." What do you mean? You condemn men to slavery, when his nature is free and possesses free will, and you legislate in competition with God, overturning His law for the human species. The one made on the specific terms that he should be the owner of the earth, and appointed to government by the Creator – him you bring under the yoke of slavery, as though defying and fighting against the divine decree. You have forgotten the limits of your authority, and that your rule is confined to control over things without reason! Why do you go beyond what is subject to you and raise yourself up against the very species which is free, counting your own kind on a level with four-footed things and even footless things?*
[You say,] "I got me slave-girls and slaves." For what price, tell me? What did you find in existence worth as much as this human nature? What price did you put on rationality? How many obols (a unit of currency) did you reckon the equivalent of the likeness of God? How many staters did you get for selling that being shaped by God? God said, Let us make man in our own image and likeness. If he is in the likeness of God, and rules the whole earth, and has been granted authority over everything on earth from God, who is his

buyer, tell me? Who is his seller? To God alone belongs this power... **God would not therefore reduce the human race to slavery, since he himself, when we had been enslaved to sin, spontaneously recalled us to freedom. But if God does not enslave what is free, who is he that sets his own power above God's?"** *(Source: Gregory of Nyssa's Homilies on Ecclessiastes. 335.5, 335.6, 336.6) 300s AD*

What a powerful challenge – and sound logical argument – from Gregory of Nyssa, who wrote the above circa 375 AD. If only the Confederate champions of slave-owning had genuinely grappled with Gregory's Scriptural and rational arguments here.

*6. For example, here are four pieces of the worldview, **all of them undermining racism.** First, at creation, all of us created in his image, all of us in his image. There are cataclysmic implications of human beings in the image of God — every kind of human being. Second sin and fall. We are one in our corruption. We are deep in solidarity in sin. You are so sinful and I am so sinful, we're right there together. There is no exalting of another above another if we are both dead-bent rebels together on our way to hell. How vain is the exaltation of self, one sinner over another sinner?*
Third, the cross. Christ died to reconcile us both talking about Jews and Gentiles at that moment — in one body to the cross, to Christ through the cross to God, or you were slain.We say to Jesus in Revelation 5:9, "You were slain and by your blood, you ransom people for God from every tribe and tongue and people and nation and you have made them a kingdom, one kingdom and priests to our God." Why? I said it's more than a social issue. Whenever I get to talk on this, I want to say to all conservative white folks who fear the social gospel, it's not a social issue. It's a blood issue. By your blood, you ransom them, all of them. You die to pull them

together, Revelation 5:9.

And fourth, faith. Not of works, and I think works means not only anything you do, but any distinctive you have does not commend you to God. Faith commends you to God and faith is a desperate I can't help myself, which puts you in line with everybody. Therefore, the way into the family is designed to remove all ethnic barriers. (Source: Pastor John Piper Sermon, Race and the Christian, preached in 2012. http://www.desiringgod.org/)

Here, in just under three minutes, pastor John Piper is able to easily and systematically undermine racism with just a few logical and Scriptural points. As Piper says, there are "cataclysmic implications" in the truth of the *Imago Dei* – that humans are made in the Image of God. One of these implications is made clear in James 3:9, **"With [the tongue] we bless our Lord and Father, and with it we curse people who are made in the likeness of God. From the same mouth come blessing and cursing. my brothers, these things ought NOT be so"** James :3:9 forbids Christians from cursing anybody with the rationale that ALL are created in the Image of God – I suggest that beating, kidnapping, and forced enslavement would also be banned under that understanding of humans being made in the *Imago Dei*.

7. The third ingredient [in love of country] is not a sentiment but a belief: a form, even prosaic belief that our own nation, in sober fact, has long been, and still is markedly superior to all others...I once ventured to say to an old clergyman who was voicing this sort of patriotism, "But, sir, aren't we told that every people thinks its own men the bravest and its own women the fairest in the world?" He replied with total gravity--he could not have been graver if he had been saying the Creed at the alter--"Yes, but in England it's true." To be sure, this conviction had not made my friend (God rest his soul) a villain; only an extremely lovable old [butt]. It can however produce [butts] that kick and bite. On the lunatic fringe it [ultra-nationalism] may shade off into that popular Racialism which Christianity and science equally forbid. (Source: C.S. Lewis, the Joyful Christian, p. 189)

Lewis is absolutely right here, if a bit colorful. Nationalism – love of country – is not always a bad thing. It can be a very good thing, but when it becomes an ultimate thing, it gets very, very ugly. It must be remembered that Christians are not first and foremost American, or English, or Laotian, or Korean…but they are first and foremost aliens and strangers in the world, citizens of Heaven. (1 Peter 2:11)

8. We are operating on illegitimate standards that are not rooted in God, but rooted in culture, rooted in history, in background. And all of that may be facts but the question we must ask is: Is it the truth? You can have facts, but it not be the truth. The truth is an objective standard by which reality is measured; it's God's point of view on any subject. Just because you were raised a certain way. Once how you were raised disagrees with what God says, how you were raised was wrong! …

If our pulpits were right we would have solved this problem of racism a long time ago. Slavery would have been solved, Jim Crow would have been solved, segregation — all of this would have been solved. But because the pulpits were anemic and allowed to take the place of the evil in America, we are still fighting that evil today! Because pulpits were silent biblically on this issue, maintaining a manifest destiny ideology that was in contrast to biblical theology! But that also explains why the Civil Rights movement was able to change it, because the church got out in front of it…

Truth overrides tradition! Truth overrides color! Black is only beautiful when it's biblical! …

You must be Christian first. If we could get enough Christians to be Christian before white, Christian before black, Christian before

155

Spanish ... it doesn't take 240 years to fix this. It takes about two minutes and 40 seconds...(Pastor Tony Evans, July 2016 sermon. Source: https://www.youtube.com/watch? v=KbhNCTJ-dUI)

Powerful words here from pastor Tony Evans. Though it is a bit of hyperbole to think we could fix racism in under three minutes, I agree that one of the things that have exacerbated racism is anti-biblical, and less than biblical, preaching on race from the pulpit.

9. These representatives of the saints in heaven are said to be around the throne. In the passage in Canticles, where Solomon sings of the King sitting at his table, some render it "a round table." From this, some expositors, I think, without straining the text, have said, "There is an equality among the saints." That idea is conveyed by the equal nearness of the four and twenty elders. The condition of glorified spirits in heaven is that of nearness to Christ, clear vision of his glory, constant access to his court, and familiar fellowship with his person: nor is there any difference in this respect between one saint and another, but all the people of God, apostles, martyrs, ministers, or private and obscure Christians, shall all be seated near the throne, where they shall for ever gaze upon their exalted Lord, and be satisfied with his love. They shall all be near to Christ, all ravished with his love, all eating and drinking at the same table with him, all equally beloved as his favourites and friends even if not all equally rewarded as servants. Let believers on earth imitate the saints in heaven in their nearness to Christ. Let us on earth be as the elders are in heaven, sitting around the throne. May Christ be the object of our thoughts, the centre of our lives C. H. Spurgeon, Morning and Evening: Daily Readings (London: Passmore & Alabaster, 1896).

Not only did Spurgeon proclaim the equality among saints, but unlike some of the Puritans (who believed the same), Spurgeon's understanding of equality among saints actually had practical implications that caused him to be an abolitionist and enemy of Victorian racism in England.

10. *Go back to 1 Timothy with me. We read over this pretty quickly when we were walking through the first part of 1 Timothy, but I want to take you back there so you can see where Paul has already addressed this kind of slavery in 1 Timothy 1. Look at 1 Timothy 1:8. We will get to it in verse 10, but see the set up. 1 Timothy 1:8–10 says,*

Now we know that the law is good, if one uses it lawfully, 9 understanding this, that the law is not laid down for the just but for the lawless and disobedient, for the ungodly and sinners, for the unholy and profane, for those who strike their fathers and mothers, for murderers, 10 the sexually immoral, men who practice homosexuality, enslavers, liars, perjurers, and whatever else is contrary to sound doctrine, (ESV)

What's the last word? "Enslavers ..." the word means literally "man stealers" or "slave dealers." Anyone who kidnaps people for sale is unholy, profane and is denying the gospel. So, I want you to see very clearly that the Bible condemns, denounces physical abuse and human trafficking. I want to emphasize that for two reasons. One, if these two truths about physical abuse and human trafficking from both testaments ... Old Testament and New Testament alike ... if these two truths had been embraced by Christians in the 18th and 19th century, slavery would never have existed like it did in the South. The Bible explicitly denounces and condemns the kind of slavery that took place in the Southern United States, and pastors and church members who used this Word to justify their practices were living in sin. (Source: David Platt, "What about Slavery, Paul?," in David Platt Sermon Archive (Birmingham, AL: David Platt, 2011), 3176.)

An excellent observation (by Southern Baptist IMB president David Platt) that Paul absolutely condemns "enslavers," which were men that took other men and forced them into slavery. As that practice was at the very heart of the chattel slavery practiced in the United States and United Kingdom, the slavery found in those countries was outlawed biblically. Tragically, Confederate pastors and many other slavery apologists chose to turn a blind eye to passages like this in the Scriptures.

11. Take away, then, directly the ornaments from women, and domestics from masters, and you will find masters in no respect different from bought slaves in step, or look, or voice, so like are they to their slaves. But they differ in that they are feebler than their slaves, and have a more sickly upbringing. For self-control is common to all human beings who have made choice of it. And we admit that the same nature exists in every race, and the same virtue. (Clement of Alexandria, around 195 AD. Source: "The Instructor," in Fathers of the Second Century: vol. 2, The Ante-Nicene Fathers (Buffalo, NY: Christian Literature Company, 1885), 280–285.)

12. What the early Christians did not have to deal with to the same extent that we do today is how race has become an idol. On both sides of the racial divide, so much is twisted by the social constructs we've formed and cling to about race...We've made a sport of pointing out racism, when what we should be doing is focusing our prayers and actions toward creating congregations that proclaim Christ's lordship over his entire church. (Source: Pastor Frank Reid (of Bethel African Methodist Episcopal Church), in Bloodlines by John Piper, 2011, p. 46)

I am not very familiar with Pastor Reid, but I agree wholeheartedly with his sentiment here. Some people seem far more interested in exacerbating racial tension by giving air to the flames, so to speak, than they do in seeking to bridge divides and come together in unity. Pointing out racism in all its forms probably does have a place, but it does not ultimately provide a solution. Being able to point out somebody's error or sin is easy, easy, easy. We are all excellent fault-finders, but fault-finding alone does not build "congregations that proclaim Christ's lordship over His entire church." If you are interested in racial harmony - and you should be - don't start by pointing out the deficiencies in other institutions. Start by having coffee with somebody and sharing Christ with them. Start by partnering in ministry with somebody. Start somewhere, but don't start with fault-finding and criticism.

*13. Many are aware of the University of Alabama's rise to football dominance under head coach Nick Saban. Less well known is the deplorable decisions made concerning their NFL-bound and 2016 National Championship MVP, O. J. Howard. **In 2011, the triple-sport athlete and top recruit was told he couldn't take his white girlfriend to prom. Yes, you read that right—in 2011.** School authorities opposed to miscegenation [inter-race relationships] didn't care about Howard's character, or that he was committed to the best college football team in the country. It only mattered that his girlfriend was white, and he was not.*

As an African American growing up in the South, one question constantly loomed over me: Whom do you belong to when you don't belong to anyone? The same black people who shamed me for excelling academically took great pride in Bill Cosby for being a doctor on The Cosby Show. What tribe do you fit in when your white girlfriend's parents prohibit their daughter from seeing you simply because of your skin color? Or when you're called "white" because your diction isn't stereotypically compatible with your ethnicity? How many brothers and sisters are too "black" to hang out with white friends and too "white" to be associated with black friends? I was caught between culture and ethnicity, trying to navigate both as rigid categories while unaware of their fluidity. So when I was called a "token," "Uncle Tom," or "house nigger," I ran from my accusers. I ran from those who looked like me.

Tokenism refers to the superficial inclusion of underrepresented groups as an attempt to dodge criticism for the organizational omission of diversity. Such a practice elicits deserved criticism, since the "token" typically doesn't possess legitimate power and is alone. His or her inclusion is an effort to satisfy criticism or mandated regulations. This kind of tokenism is unhelpful and perfunctory. However, social entrepreneurship occurs when one dares to step out into the chasm, grabs his tools, and begin to build bridges. The inclusion of minorities in decision-making positions doesn't happen overnight. Minorities operating in hegemonic spaces won't make up for decades of disproportionate hiring practices, omissions of minority pastors in homogenous churches, or segregationist leadership in secondary education. But they can be a catalyst for change. Tokenism is truly redefined when someone whose seemingly cursory hire pays it forward by generating opportunities for minorities to surpass his or her success. What many refer to as tokenism, I call pioneering. Someone has to be the first.

When O.J. Howard's mother decided to put her son in an all-white segregation-era private school, whites and blacks alike criticized her. But when her son was unjustly discriminated, the entire community rallied to their aid. The Howards stepped into the chasm and gave the Autauga Academy community the gift of going second. Perhaps a black man was given the gift of going second in that church I preached in, too. Redefining tokenism isn't a call to strip away ethnicity or culture in order to recognize the humanity in a systemically dehumanized soul. It's a call of encouragement to those who don't have the luxury of walking on worn paths. Redefining tokenism is for those with a machete in hand, blazing a trail for all who will come behind that back-breaking work. What begins as a goat path may soon become a highway. Someone has to be first.

I don't think Paul had to endure the requests of strangers to touch his hair, or someone asking if he gets sunburned after standing in the sun too long. But he did give us the gift of going second by suffering for the sake of Christ (2 Tim. 2:10). Countless believers have looked on his tumult, hardships, and scars and found camaraderie. With every church he planted, city he was thrown out of, and conversion he praised God for, Paul cleared a path for the gospel of grace to bear fruit in the world. Paul pioneered ministry among the Gentiles, suffering for our sake, so that we could be included in the family of God. (Source: www.thegospelcoalition.org/article/the-gift-of-going-second)

You should read this whole article from pastor Jason Cook, who is located in Memphis, but went to school at the same seminary I did. It is equal parts inspiring and challenging, and is a needed word for the church of today. As an Alabama fan, I had no idea that O.J. Howard endured the racism that he did in high school.

14. God has a kingdom. It's made up of citizens. Some black, some white, some red, yellow, Spanish backgrounds. His intention was never that the individual uniqueness would cause them to lose sight of the flag flying over them. The flag of the cross ... America in particular is reaching an all-time low in this issue of race and culture and class. Just under the surface there is this ever-bubbling problem that has gone unresolved...

We have voices about which life matters. All life is created in the image of God. All lives matter. However, underneath the banner that God has created all people in his image, there are inequities that must be addressed. For example, the life of the unborn matters. And so there is this emphasis on injustice in the womb. But that injustice in the womb must be under the umbrella that all life matters. Black lives matter, as a subset of all lives matter. So any injustices to a particular group must be addressed specific to that group but under the banner that all life is created in the image of God...(Pastor Tony Evans, Summer 2016 Sermon, "A Biblical Response on Race" Source: https://www.youtube.com/watch?v=KbhNCTJ-dUI)

Another excellent word from pastor Tony Evans. The whole message is worth watching, and can be viewed on Youtube.

15. The Bible clearly teaches that all mankind is derived from Noah and his three sons. Noah's three sons' names were Shem, Ham and Japheth (Genesis 9:18). The International Standard Bible Encyclopedia, 1956 Edition, states that the word Ham means "dark or black," Shem means "dusky or olive-colored," and Japheth means "bright or fair."
Biblical scholars, and at least one prominent anthropologist, consider Ham to be the ancestral father of Negroes, Mongoloids and Indians; Shem is considered to be the ancestral father of Semites (Arabic and Jewish); and Japheth is considered to be the ancestral father of Caucasians. Are the scholars correct? Based on the etymology of the three sons' names, the nations associated with these names in Genesis 10, historical research and biblical data, I'm inclined to agree with the scholars: Noah's three sons were the progenitors of the three basic races of mankind. I was puzzled though as to how could a monogamous Noah produce three sons of three different complexions, and, consequently, ethnic identities. This seemed biologically impossible to me. I was forced to consider the ethnicity of Adam and Eve.
Vince Lombardi was a fanatic for fundamentals. And when the

Green Bay Packers lost two games that they should have easily won, Vince Lombardi called his men in for a special session, held a football high in the air, and said, "Men, this is a football." I've simply come to say, this is the Bible. The Bible is the inerrant and infallible Word of God. And the Word of God says in Genesis 2:7, "God formed man from the dust of the ground..."

Dirt comes in a wide variety of colors, but it usually has a color component to it. The name Adam in Hebrew means "red" or taken out of red earth. The name "Adam" is also translated "man." Adam was the first human. The prefix "hu" in "human" means color. Adam, made from dirt, was a man of color." He and Eve possessed the genetic capacity to produce all of the colors you see on the face of the earth today.

Therefore, with all of us descending from one common origin, we must be unified. We all can trace our roots back to Ham, Shem, Japheth, Noah and Adam. That makes us one family.

*** We must be unified because Jesus said His Kingdom missionary agenda is intertwined with His followers being in unity (John 17:21).

*** We must be unified because Acts 2:1 is clear that the Holy Spirit descended when the church was unified.

*** We must be unified because the Psalmist said it's a beautiful picture, and blessings flow when God's people are unified (Psalm 133:1-3).

*** We must be unified because we cannot stand against the wiles of the devil, if we are not in unity. Jesus said, "And if a house is divided against itself, that house cannot stand" (Mark 3:25).

*** We must be unified because the church cannot defeat the Alt-Right unless we are unified (Ephesians 6:10-12).

*** We must be unified, now.

The early church was unified (Acts 13:1), and the hand of the Lord was upon them (Acts 11:21). They were a multi-ethnic church in a multi-ethnic city—"and a great number believed, and turned to *the Lord."*

*During the days of slavery, a woman became temporarily sep-
arated from her fairly newborn baby on a very large cotton
plantation. After many hours of unsuccessfully searching for the
child, the idea was suggested that all the workers should join hands
and walk down each row until they found the baby.*

*Sure enough, this method worked. But when they found the baby,
the baby was lifeless, dead, because of the many hours in the sun
without water. Someone then remarked, had we joined hands
earlier, we could have saved the baby. My brothers and sisters, if
the White Church, Black Church, Hispanic Church and Asian Church
join hands, we can save America. If we join hands, we can defeat
the Alt-Right. If we join hands we can show the world a beautiful
picture and win the world for Christ together. Jesus said, "And I,
if I am lifted up from the earth, will draw all peoples to Myself."
(John 12:32)*

Source: https://dwightmckissic.wordpress.com

I praise God for pastor and writer Dwight Mckissic and his willingness,
for the sake of Jesus' call to oneness, to suffer significant derision
from both sides of the racial divide. He has a prophetic voice in the
Southern Baptist church, and woe unto our denomination if we take
steps that might drive him, and others like him, away.

*16. While under terrible pressure from all that is happening around
us, we must persevere with obedience to the Christian ethic. People
are very angry in Sri Lanka these days as the country deteriorates
into more and more lawlessness and abuse. Many have given up
hope, and their despair is expressing itself in outbursts of anger
(e.g. on the road). But we cannot burst out angrily like that for
Christian love is always patient (1 Cor. 13:4). We are seeing a lot
of impoliteness especially in workplaces. But Christian love is not
rude (1 Cor. 13:5). People are rejected and spoken to as terrorist*

suspects simply because of the race they belong to.
But such racial profiling contradicts Christian love which believes
all things and hopes all things (1 Cor. 13:7). People are giving up on
Sri Lanka and leaving even though millions in this nation desper-
ately need Jesus and Sri Lanka desperately needs people of integrity
in public life. Such flight contradicts Christian love which endures
all things (1 Cor. 13:7). One of the greatest challenges Christians
face in this fast paced, competitive, impatient, results-oriented,
appearance-fixated world is being thoroughgoing followers of the
Christian ethic all the time. (Ajith Fernando, "Sovereignty, Prayer
and Perseverance" at AjithFernando.com)

Ajith Fernando is an evangelist and writer from Sri Lanka. In the
above quote, he is describing the racial disquiet that was shaking his
home country in 2008. Notice how similar it is to the situation that
Americans have faced over the past few years, and consider even more
Ajith's call to remain in places of great upheaval, a call that seriously
questions a "white flight" mindset.

15

Interactive Book: YOU Write the Last Chapter

This space is reserved for YOU. The beauty of independent publishing is that I can very easily add content to my books after they are published. Going forward, the plan is to have an interactive chapter in almost every book I write so that this space can be used to interact with readers by responding to questions, criticisms and comments. I would love to hear from you! Please contact me with your take on this book. What did I miss – what should have been included? Where was I wrong, either in tone, or in content? What did you agree with? What was encouraging to you? What racial or ethnic perspective did I miss or under-represent? Please contact me through my webpage: www.Chaseathompson.com/blog or just email me at: Chaseathompson@gmail.com

Within a few months of publication, I intend to include a whole extra chapter of interactive material in this section. It will be a free Kindle update, and will be available on my website for those that have bought the print version of the book.

16

Appendix: A Meditation on White Privilege

T he following is an edited and updated article that appeared on
my writing blog, www.Chaseathompson.com, in 2016, right
around the time that Philando Castile was shot and killed by a
police officer.

I have come to understand that most white people do not understand
what it is like to be a person of color and engage with law enforcement.
Approximately twelve years ago I had a week where there was a
warrant out for my arrest, and my driver's license was suspended.
During that one week period, even though it was illegal, I continued
to drive to work. And was pulled over one day by a policeman. While
I had an illegal weapon under my front seat. Below, I will tell the
story of that encounter, and how it ultimately ended, but first, a few
preliminaries.

Here is my disclaimer: I get that I am a white guy writing about
racial issues, and that, in doing so, I am writing about a very, very
sensitive issue that I don't fully understand. I have tried to be slow to
react to things, and slow to write about them, because there is wisdom
in not being hasty. I am not a wise man, but I want to be. As the Word
says, "Everyone should be quick to listen, slow to speak, and slow

to become angry." (James 1:19) I wanted to write about this subject extensively last Thursday and Friday – partially because it would have gotten more clicks (stupid motivation, I know), but also because I had strong opinions about what everybody was saying online! However – I felt chastened to be quick to LISTEN. SLOW to speak and SLOW to become angry.

My contributions to the issue of racial harmony and race issues in general will be quite limited. Partially because I am a white man, and I have rarely (if ever) been the victim of some kind of discrimination based on my skin color. Partially because I come from relative affluence. Partially because I just can't see the overall big picture. That said – I want to try. I want to try and understand. I want to try and contribute. I want to try and "Make every effort to maintain the unity of the Spirit through the bond of peace." (Ephesians 4:3) There will be things over the next few posts that I get wrong, but I hope that they will be sincere errors – made by a man who is trying to understand and striving to be faithful biblically. One other thing: I love law enforcement, and spent my much of my entire life, even into graduate school, planning on becoming an FBI or DEA agent. I even spent time at the University of Alabama Criminal Justice graduate school to prepare for a career in law enforcement. I will write more about this in a later post, but despite my love and respect for law enforcement, I do not blindly support the police. Neither do I blindly support Baptists, or preachers, or husbands, or fathers, or Alabama football fans, even though I am part of all of those categories. More on that later...

In July of 2016, Russell Moore, one of the key Southern Baptist leaders, wrote something that is actually fairly radical (for a Southern Baptist):

Many white evangelicals will point to specific cases, and argue that the particulars are more complex in those situations than initial news reports might show. But how can anyone deny, after seeing the sheer number of cases and after seeing those in which the situation is all too clear, that there is a problem in terms of the safety of African-Americans before the law. That's especially true when one considers the history of a country in which African-Americans have lived with trauma from the very beginning, the initial trauma being the kidnapping and forced enslavement of an entire people with no standing whatsoever before the law. For the black community, these present situations often reverberate with a history of state-sanctioned violence, in a way that many white Americans—including white evangelicals—often don't understand. (Source: http://www.russellmoore.com/)

Dr. Moore's comment that is so striking, and a bit odd to hear from a Southern Baptist, is this one, "there is a problem in terms of the safety of African-Americans before the law." Without accusing any particular group of racism, I believe that Dr. Moore is correct in that assessment, and so do many of my Christian black friends. It is an inarguable statistical fact that unarmed black males are shot by law enforcement at a disproportional rate relative to their population size – over six times that which mathematics alone would seem to indicate. As the Washington Post has noted (see below) black males account for 40 percent of all unarmed men shot by police in 2015, but only make up 6 percent of the population. While the majority of people in America shot by police were indeed white, the majority (60 percent) of people that were shot while "exhibiting less than threatening behavior" were black or Hispanic. If I was black or Hispanic, speaking frankly, this would alarm me.

Although black men make up only 6 percent of the U.S. population, they account for 40 percent of the unarmed men shot to death by police this year, The Post's database shows. In the majority of cases in which police shot and killed a person who had attacked someone with a weapon or brandished a gun, the person who was shot was white. But a hugely disproportionate number — 3 in 5 — of those killed after

THE BIBLE AND RACISM

exhibiting less threatening behavior were black or Hispanic. (Source: Washington Post)

Twelve years ago, I was a youth pastor that made about $600 a week (when my church salary and part time work were combined), and was supporting a family of five on that income. Some weeks the offering was lower than others, and we would only get a partial paycheck, or no paycheck that week. These are some of the realities of working in a church situation. This particular year, our finances crumbled quite a bit. I ended up having my truck repossessed, and got into some pretty bad credit card debt. Not wise! In the midst of that, I let the payments on my car insurance lapse, and was pulled over by a police officer for a tail light issue. I didn't get a ticket for the tail light issue, but I did get a ticket for driving without insurance. I paid the insurance and got current, but then FORGOT about paying the ticket, until one week after it was due. I finally realized my irresponsible error when I got a notice from the Trussville City Hall that a warrant had been issued for my arrest and my driver's license had been suspended! That was a shocking experience for a guy who still pined for a life in law enforcement from time to time. I called my dad, the lawyer, and he instructed me to call the court and throw myself at their mercy. They told me that a hearing was scheduled in about 10 days (roughly) and that I would need to come and plead my case before a judge, which I agreed to do.

Unfortunately, my driver's license was still suspended, and I didn't have a good way to get to work. So I drove. One afternoon after work, as I was driving home, I got pulled over by another police officer, but I don't remember why. I think it was for failure to fully stop at a stop sign, but I don't remember the exact context. Whatever it was, when I noticed the blue lights behind me, I froze in panic. Not panic FOR MY LIFE...but because I knew I was in trouble. When the office came up to the car, the first thing I said was something like, "I am sorry sir...I am driving with a suspended license." Of course, he began to eye me suspiciously, and I explained what happened. He then asked me, "Do you have any weapons in your car?" I told him that I had a knife under my front seat, and he asked to see it. I, without any thought of being in danger whatsoever, reached under my front seat and pulled out a knife with a sixteen inch blade.

I guess I should offer an explanation about why I drove around with a knife under my front seat, and why I still do. I should have a good reason for that, but I don't really have a decent rationale. I guess it is just in case I am in a car-jacking situation, or terrorists try to invade the country and commandeer my car. When that happens, I will be ready with my trusty knife under the front seat. Terrorists and carjackers...Beware!

Anyway, I pulled out the knife and handed it to him. His eyes got kind of big, then narrowed at me. "Sir, did you know that you can't have a blade longer than ten (?) inches in the front of your car?!" Actually, no, I did not know that at the time, but apparently it was either a Hoover, Alabama ordinance, or a state law, or whatever. Now, I was about to be busted for rolling through a stop sign, driving with a suspended license, AND having an illegal weapon under my front seat. I was sweating and extremely nervous by now, but at no time did it ever cross my mind that this police officer was about to hit me, hurt me, or shoot me. I just figured it would be a big-honking ticket that was about to come my way...maybe even a "ride down to the station."

Ultimately, for whatever reason, the police officer displayed unusual mercy, and let me go without a ticket, or a tasing, or anything like that. I had to call a friend to come pick me up, because the officer wouldn't let me drive, but other than that there were no further tickets or ramifications for what I had done. Most of my experiences with law enforcement have been this way. Law enforcement has always been fair with me...and sometimes overly fair and merciful.

Is that the essence of what some call "white privilege?" Perhaps so – I imagine that it is part of it, at least. I take it for granted that when I have encounters with law enforcement, that I am not about to get shot at or beaten up, unless I have done something that deserves such treatment.

My black friends, however, have a radically different perspective than I do. These friends – pastors, teachers, counselors, professionals – tell me stories of being pulled over for no good reason. They tell me that they are often afraid of law enforcement – as in physically afraid. That is not my experience, but I do not want to cheapen their experience by failing to understand it, or empathize. I have come to hear of that perception from my black friends enough to believe that it is not merely bias, but that it has a basis in fact. I believe, as mentioned earlier, that white people either deny this reality, or they are blissfully unaware of it. I believe that must change in order for our churches, our neighborhoods and our countries to achieve a higher level of racial harmony.

To those who deny the premise of this article – that white people have a different experience with law enforcement than most minorities – allow me to ask you a question and offer you a challenge. Have you ever talked frankly with some of your black and Hispanic friends about their views of law enforcement? Not just one or two, but enough to get a good picture of what those in your relational circle actually think, and have experienced. If you have not done this, then please let me encourage you to do so. Ask in a non-argumentative way, and just listen. You might be surprised at the answers you hear, and they might be surprised that you care....and that is a good start towards "seeking peace and pursuing it." (1 Peter 3:11) This whole situation is not about winning an argument, or being right, or scoring political points in your social media posts. It is about real, live human beings who are hurting, angry, confused, and struggling. Blessed are the peacemakers, says Jesus. Be one!

You will likely note in this post that I am attempting to take both "sides." That is a true observation, though I completely deny the "us vs. them" narrative. This issue is not ultimately about minorities vs. law enforcement, though there are conflicting powers that would frame it that way. Ultimately, I myself side with law enforcement,

AND I side with minorities who are afraid of law enforcement. You might accuse me of playing both sides of the fence, but I will, over the next few articles on race, try to make the case that understanding both sides of this issue and being in favor of each one is the only rational, logical and triumphant position to take in this situation. All other positions are doomed to failure and increasing divisiveness. Along those lines, I'll close with some compelling and powerful words from Dr. Brian Williams, whom you might note ALSO chooses to side with law enforcement AND his fellow brothers and sisters that are fearful of law enforcement.

Dr. Brian Williams is a trauma surgeon in Dallas. He was on duty at the emergency room the night Micah Johnson murdered several Dallas law enforcement people. CNN interviewed him this week, and I find myself in wholehearted agreement with much of what he said:

> *"I'm thinking about the officers and their families and the men that were killed in Baton Rouge and Minnesota last week and I compare my situation to theirs and it's hard for me to focus on myself right now. I don't understand why people think its OK to kill police officers. I don't understand why black men die in custody and they're forgotten the next day. I don't know why this has to be us against them. This is all really... it has to stop. We are all in this together, we are all connected. All this violence, all this hatred, all these disagreements, it impacts us all, whether you realize it or not. This is not the kind of world we want to leave for our children. Something has to be done."*

> *"Clearly when I'm at work dressed in my white coat the reactions I get with individuals and the officers I deal with on a daily basis are much different than what I would get outside the hospital in regular clothes and my fear and mild inherent distrust in law enforcement, that goes back to my own personal experiences that I've had in my own personal life as well as hearing the stories from friends and family that look like me, that have had*

similar experiences," he said. "I work with (law enforcement) on a daily basis; they're my colleagues, they're my friends, and I respect what they do. But I also understand how men like me can fear and distrust officers in uniform. "I get it, but that does not justify inciting violence against police officers. It does not justify trying to kill police officers. This incident [the shooting of police officers] didn't fix anything; it's making it worse." (Source: http://www.cnn.com/2016/07/11/ us/emotional-dallas-dr-williams/index.html)

17

Appendix B: The Deadly Danger of Outrage

Imagine a scene where a group of people are on the side of a mountain during a disaster – perhaps a plane crash of some sort – and there is a large group of survivors. Unfortunately, the survivors are in a perilous position – there is the danger of avalanche, and they are high atop a precarious perch. Further imagine that initially some of the survivors panic and start running around and hollering and causing trouble. In a desperate situation, those people – the loudest, angriest and most frightened – are rarely, if ever, part of the solution. They are often, however, part of the problem.

In the United States right now, we are in a bit of a crisis situation, somewhat analogous to our friends who have survived the plane crash above. There is a simmering sort of tension right now between minorities and law enforcement, and racial tension itself seems to on the rise in a way that I can't remember seeing in the past two decades.

So here we have a powder keg of a situation that has all interested parties in a state of nervous agitation – not a good place to be for an armed populace, and an armed constabulary. What is the ROOT cause here? By that question, I am actually asking the question: "What is the ROOT cause of the CURRENT/RECENT inflamed racial situation involving minorities, law enforcement, and the whole nation? Is it racism in law enforcement? While that could ultimately be a contributing factor, I don't actually believe it is the overall cause, although I freely admit that there are racists (of many stripes) running about in law enforcement, and in literally every segment of society: business, hospitals, churches, etc.

Is the current root cause perhaps that anti-law enforcement aggression and anger exhibited by such groups as #BlackLivesMatter is contributing towards an atmosphere that is leading to a greater level of aggression and defensiveness from police officers? Again – I do not believe that to be the ROOT cause, though I do believe that some wings and groups within the umbrella of BLM do indeed seem to produce some excessively inflammatory rhetoric that could well be inciting violence and hatred at times.

That said, from my very limited and imperfect perspective, I don't think that racism is currently on the rise in America the way it seems to be. I DO think we are more enlightened and less racist now than when we were in the sixties and seventies. That was a different time, it seems to me, than it is today. When I was eight years old (in the early 1980s), I had a friend named Alex Coleman – a Black guy. He was one of my best friends, and he would occasionally come over to play with me at our family's house in a relatively affluent white suburb. (Vestavia Hills, Alabama)

I have never forgotten the time that my dad hung up the phone one evening at our house, and informed me that the caller was a neighbor who was irate that I was playing with a black boy outside in full view of all of the other neighbors. Apparently that wasn't the only time that such complaining phone calls happened. I was bewildered about such ignorant, stupid hatred then, and I am bewildered about it now. But I believe that we are seeing less and less of that kind of attitude in this country.

Is Racism a core part of the problem in the increasing tensions between minorities and law enforcement? Yes – it absolutely is. I believe there is probably more racism that is active in the country now than most white people would believe and/or acknowledge. (And possibly less than some race agitators, social justice warriors and other strife-causers might admit) I also believe that there is a fairly substantial amount of racial hatred directed by minorities towards whites, and other different minority groups. Bottom line: There is enough racial animus in our country that we should all be ashamed and repent in humility and sackcloth and ashes. But nobody is really denying that part of our problem is race. And I don't think that racism is actually on the INCREASE. I think that there is something else that is fueling the recent racial strife that has been making headlines over the past few years. I blame YOU. (and ME too, actually)

See if you can follow me on this. I'm going to present a theory. I don' t think it is especially new or novel, but I don't hear many commentators speaking about it on the news, and I haven't read many writers who have discusses it in depth. I believe that the MEDIA is responsible for a surprisingly high proportion of the current, ongoing racial strife. Now – DON'T stop reading yet. I don't mean merely mean the MAINSTREAM media...I am actually MORE referring to US – We The People; We The Social Media.

The bottom line – I think the media, and especially social media, is causing a vicious circle that is leading to an atmosphere of fear, distrust and separation in America that is ultimately fueling violent action, and divisive arguments. Note that I am not blaming the faceless "mainstream media," or the "liberal media," or the "conservative media," or whatever. I am blaming US.

Remember our plane crash illustration above? Sometimes the loudest, most agitated and most panicked people in a given situation can cause trouble and strife and danger for the whole group. Given a situation where a group of survivors are huddled on a mountainside, if a few people panic or get alarmed, or jump up and run around screaming – disaster could happen to everybody. Likewise, in a social media climate where so many people are ANGRY and ATTACKING...I believe we are creating a similar dynamic in our country. Social media is so ubiquitous and ANGER and RAGE on social media is so common, that most of us are getting a daily dose of it. And I don' t believe it is helping; I believe it is incredibly harmful to us as society. Not social media itself – but OUTRAGE and SLANDER and ATTACKS (of each other and whatever groups we don't like) on social media.

I believe the Bible actually has something powerful and profound to say to us right now, as a country. It is a warning and a glorious encouragement:

> *Galatians 5:13-15 For you were called to be free, brothers; only don't use this freedom as an opportunity for the flesh, but serve one another through love. For the entire law is fulfilled in one statement: Love your neighbor as yourself. But if you bite and devour one another, watch out, or you will be consumed by one another.*

We are at our highest as people when we are loving each other the way that we want to be loved. This is the Golden Rule of Jesus found in Matthew 7:12. How do you want to be loved by people? Do you enjoy being attacked, or belittled? Do you enjoy when people take your point of view and twist it into a caricature of what you actually believe, and then make it appear that you support something that you would never agree with? Do you enjoy being fussed at or accused of being abusive or being racist? Probably not...therefore, be exceedingly careful about avoiding doing that with others. If WE aren't careful about that, then the Apostle Paul's warning above will be true of us: If we keep on biting and devouring each other, we will eventually implode, and there will be nothing left. And I believe that is what is happening in our country.

So – here's my encouragement: Stop attacking people...even when you are sure they are wrong. Think about it for a moment: When was the last time your opinion on something was changed by somebody who was insulting you in an overbearing or critical or negative way? All of us have been berated in the past to change our opinion, but that change of opinion – even when we were moving closer to the truth – was often an overall negative experience when it was initiated in a negative way. And decisions made that way don't often stick. I'm not saying don't confront racism. I'm saying don't be an outraged jerk who is constantly castigating groups or people who don't see things exactly the way you do. Do you want to spread truth? Good – me too! How should we do that?

I don't think there has ever been a person better at persuading people of truth than Jesus Christ Himself. I believe His approach is the same type of approach we should use. A humble approach. A servant-focused approach. A self-sacrificing approach. You might think that sounds too weak – or too passive. But it is not – Not even close – Jesus was neither weak nor passive, and His message has endured world wide for almost 2000 years. Nobody has ever spoken a more powerful and enduring message than Jesus. We should be like Him. How did He do it? I conclude part two of this five part series with a meditation on Jesus' approach to saving the world and teaching and spreading His truth from the Apostle Paul, in Philippians, chapter 2:

> *Do nothing out of rivalry or conceit, but in humility consider others as more important than yourselves. Everyone should look out not only for his own interests, but also for the interests of others. Make your own attitude that of Christ Jesus, who, existing in the form of God, did not consider equality with God as something to be used for His own advantage. Instead He emptied Himself by assuming the form of a slave, taking on the likeness of men. And when He had come as a man in His external form, He humbled Himself by becoming obedient to the point of death— even to death on a cross.*
>
> *For this reason God highly exalted Him and gave Him the name that is above every name, so that at the name of Jesus every knee will bow— of those who are in heaven and on earth and under the earth and every tongue should confess that Jesus Christ is*

Lord, to the glory of God the Father.

18

Appendix C: Facebook Flogging and False Alarms

The article below was written for my website, chaseathompson.com, during the Summer of 2016. There was a similar controversy during the Summer of 2017, when many voices on social media called for ESPN to denounce a fantasy football segment that featured players being auctioned off to imaginary team 'owners.' Shaun King, a writer, tweeted the following:

Dear @ESPN, Apologize now for doing a sketch where you auctioned a Black man off to the highest bidder. https://twitter.com/shaunking/status/897445750317219840

The problem with King's tweet and the flurry of controversy that followed is that there is nothing at all racial about the fantasy football practice of 'auctioning' players. It is simply one of the many ways that football nerds, of which I am one, can assemble their team at the beginning of the year. The 'auction' format means that, rather than drafting players turn by turn, players of fantasy football bid a certain amount to acquire a player for their imaginary team. Players of all kinds are drafted in this manner - Hispanic, Asian, white, black, etc. Shaun King's tweet made it appear that the focus of the segment was to "auction off a black man to the highest bidder," but that wasn't the case at all. All players, of all races, were included in this segment, based on an imaginary fantasy football team.

Ultimately, I don't believe that crying foul on things like this is helpful at all towards racial harmony. In fact, I believe that King's complaints over this segment, and Lebron James' suggestion, detailed below, that Phil Jackson was racist for using the word "posse," are counterproductive, and produce a rise in racial acrimony, rather than racial unity. **Demanding apologies for things that aren't actually racist is confusing**. Racism must be denounced, but innocent things like the use of the word "posse," and fantasy football auctions should probably be left alone. What do you think?

Allow me to start off with a provoking statement, and then walk it back a little bit later: *LeBron James was a whiny millennial this week that actually deepened racial divides with his rebuke of Phil Jackson, and probably left a lot of people clueless about how to actually come together racially in this country.* Characterizing benign, un-racist comments as racist sows confusion, and effectively leads to an overall net increase in racism. For the full comments from Jackson, and Lebron's response, scroll down to the bottom of this post, just under the Youtube video of LeBron's interview.

As you can read in the comments below (at the very bottom of this chapter) During the Summer of 2016, NBA superstar LeBron James took exception to Hall of Fame Coach Phil Jackson labeling LeBron's business partners as "his posse." To James, the use of the word "posse" was highly offensive and had racial overtones:

"To use that label and if you go and read the definition of what the word 'posse' is, it's not what I've built over my career," James said. "It's not what I stand for, it's not what my family stands for. I believe the only reason he used that word is because he sees young African-Americans trying to make a difference." – LeBron James

Technically, James is correct. The textbook definition of "posse" is:

"1. A group of people who were gathered together by a sheriff in the past to help search for a criminal. 2. A group of people who are together for a particular purpose. 3. A group of friends" (Merriam-Webster Dictionary online dictionary)

If Jackson is intending to imply that LeBron's friends were gathered by the sheriff to search for a criminal, then I guess that would probably be inaccurate, but not racially offensive. Likewise, the other two definitions seem very benign as well. And yet, many people thousands of people, including former NBA star Reggie Miller, consider Jackson's words as racist, and writer Victoria Uwumarogie goes so far as to say:

"I do think it's a shame that such language is used when speaking on young men of color who are doing great things."

I would agree with LeBron and Reggie and Victoria if, in fact, the use of the word "posse" had some sort of racial or negative connotations. The trouble is, that it doesn't. And I don't think it is fair to just pick a word, or phrase, or idea, and then all of the sudden assign negative racial overtones to it, and then attack people for using it. Below, I want to consider two things highly relative to the use of the word "posse," and how we handle offense (particularly racial offense), in this country. First, an analysis of whether the word "posse" should be considered offensive or not, followed by a few words on handling offense in a healthy, peace-making way.

When I hear "posse," I think of western style cowboys going after criminals. It would never cross my mind that the word has some sort of racial overtones. How is this actually an offensive word? I remember the first time, a couple of years ago, that I began to realize that the word "thug" had come to carry with it racial overtones. That initially surprised me, but nobody would disagree that "thug" is an unpleasant word that is not meant to be a positive characterization of whomever it is applied to, so I can understand that word being offensive to African American groups (as well as those from India, where the word actually originated.) Posse, however, seems to be a word that actually has positive connotations, not negative ones, and I can find scant etymological evidence of the word being used in a disparaging way in recent history. Indeed, here are some examples:

1. The New York Times, in 2007, refers to Senate Majority Leader Mitch McConnell and his Posse. (For reference, McConnell, a white guy, was 65 at the time.)

2. Mother Jones, in 2012, writes about presidential candidate Mitt Romney and his posse here.

3. Michael Jones, in Newsweek, writes about 80 year senator old Jesse Helms, and his posse, here in 2001.

4. At Salon.com, Heather Parton writes of Donald Trump and his posse in October of 2016.

5. Similarly, At Nuvo, Stephanie Dolan makes reference to George W. Bush and his posse in September of 2015.

6. Keeping with the old white guy theme, Cnet.com makes multiple references over the years to Bill Gates and his posse, including this one, from 2008.

7. Another use of posse referencing old white guys, by Ilana Mercer in World News Daily, discusses Rudy Giuliani and his posse.

8. Though he is not actually real, the U.S. News and World Reports magazine does reference Ronald McDonald and his posse.

9. Sarah Wolfe, writing for PRI.org, makes mention of Warren Buffet and his posse.

10. And finally, did you know that Thomas Jefferson had a posse? Well, thanks to writer Tony Jones, you do now.

11. A few years before Phil Jackson did it, African American sportswriter Ron Glover wrote about LeBron and his "posse," and nobody seemed to understand that word as having racial undertones.

Note: You can find links to all of the above articles at my website, www.Chaseathompson.com.

Bottom line, as evidenced above, there is scant (if any) evidence of "posse" being used as a consistently derogatory or racially loaded term prior to November of 2016. I suppose now, going forward, that the use of this word will change, which is fine with me. The point I wish to make here is that there is little, if any, evidence supporting the use of this word as a racial code word of some kind, and as such – we should be very careful about raising a false alarm. The problem with false alarms is that the more they are raised, the less meaningful true alarms become. I believe the way to change the climate of our country for the better in terms of race relations is not to confront benign activities but to reveal racial heart-hatreds and genuine prejudices and deal strongly with those!

Here's my big question – how are people of differing races to know what words, phrases or ideas are offensive to other cultures? Is there a big list somewhere? I think racism requires heart intent and prejudice. In other words, somebody could actually use the word "posse" in a derogatory way that is meant to wound, slander, or denigrate another race, and somebody else could use the word in a completely innocent sense. The key with these sorts of neutral words is the heart and attitude that lies behind their use. The danger in what LeBron has apparently done here (implicitly accuse somebody of racism for using a demonstrably benign word) is that it actually creates the kind of atmosphere where racism and genuine racist language can flourish. How? Because of the Boy Who Cried Wolf Syndrome. Do you remember the old nursery tale about that boy? He was a shepherd watching sheep, and, for whatever reason, he raised a false alarm about wolves attacking multiple times. When an actual wolf appeared and began doing damage – nobody listened to his cries of alarm! Similarly, when language use is so scrutinized that we get upset and offended over demonstrably benign utterances, then it is possible that many people will ignore the noise when actual racist language is used.

Bullying is a big cultural enemy right now. When I was young, a bully was somebody that physically threatened or intimidated you in a frightening way. That word has expanded its meaning exponentially today, so that people are declaring themselves bullied over a wide variety of issues. The trouble with that is that the original meaning of the word is actually watered down quite a bit. When every act can be interpreted as bullying, then the word loses its power and NOTHING is bullying. When everybody gets a trophy for participating, then the value of a trophy actually goes down. It's simple economics. Similarly, when the hue and cry of racism is voiced loudly and often (in the seeming absence of true racism), then people become numb and deaf to it – and that is a terrible, terrible danger! Racism is a terrible evil, and it should be confronted powerfully. Benign use of words, however, should not be labeled as racism, nor intimated to be racist.

Addressing our shared culture right now is like stepping through a mine field. It is incredibly difficult to know how to avoid offending every subculture and group. I am not sure that is the best way for a society built on liberty to function. Part of the reason for the rise of Trump and his surprising election win could be, that In a climate where people get offended at pretty much everything, at some point, somebody is going to throw up their hands and stop caring that their speech and actions offend everybody. Donald Trump said multiple offensive things during the presidential campaign, and there were several offensive statements that he said previously that also came out during the campaign. In the past, those statements would have been enough to shut down his presidential bid, and he would have resigned from the race. In 2016, not only did that not happen, but Trump actually pulled off an upset win. This, despite the fact that the news media almost everywhere decried him as a sexist, racist, misogynist, and plenty of other "ists." Why didn't this end his campaign? Why did people vote for him? Was it because a majority of white Americans are racists? Possibly, but I want to offer a second theory: In a culture with so many accusations of sexism and racism and misogyny, is it possible that those words have lost their power to condemn because of situations like these? It could be we are dealing with The Boy Who Cried Wolf Syndrome. How do we change that? – I would suggest that the best way to change it is to only cry wolf when there is an actual wolf.

When everything is offensive speech then what? Do we stop talking to each other? Do we walk around on egg shells? Do we think so much about every word that we become stiff and wooden? When we get THIS offended by everything that could be possibly interpreted as a slur(racial/sexual/religion/body-type/gender, etc) then the people that really are hard-core racists and awful people are essentially cloaked and hidden in with everybody else. Is Phil Jackson a racist? Well – he IS an old white man...does that make him a racist? I don't think so. Well, he did use the word "posse" – does that make him a racist?! Does that make him somebody who is using "coded language?" I guess that is possible, but highly unlikely. I guarantee that Phil will take the word "posse" out of his everyday vocabulary, but has good been done in dragging his name through the mud? I doubt it. Rather than strengthen racial reconciliation as a whole in this country, I suspect that this episode has caused resentment, confusion and anything but racial harmony. I don't want to be complicit with that in this article – I just want to sound a somewhat muted alarm that we should be careful about veiled accusations of racism targeted towards people who aren't, in fact racists.

I'll close the main part of this article with a solution that is based on Jesus' teaching on peacemaking from Matthew 18. If LeBron was genuinely offended by Jackson's use of the word "posse." How should he have handled it? I think he should have gone to Phil Jackson first, in private. Maybe a phone call or a text message. There's no doubt in my mind that LeBron would have any difficulty in getting a message to Jackson. I don't know how Jackson would have received such a message, but I imagine that he might well have apologized to LeBron for unintentionally wounding him, and that would have been a good thing. Maybe we should all consider handling offenses the way that Jesus suggested! Rather than immediately airing our offense out, or pointing fingers of accusation, or vague-booking...maybe a simple text, or email, or what have you might be just the thing that would lead towards peace. And I am a fan of peace!

1 Peter 3:10-12 "Whoever would love life and see good days must keep their tongue from evil and their lips from deceitful speech. 11 They must turn from evil and do good; they must seek peace and pursue it. 12 For the eyes of the Lord are on the righteous and his ears are attentive to their prayer, but the face of the Lord is against those who do evil"

Virtueish Signaling: Most white people begin these kind of stories with some kind of language to indicate that they aren't racists in any way. Part of me would like to do that, but the fact of the matter is that, in some ways, I am sinfully racist. I don't want to be. I really have no idea where those areas might be and how they might manifest themselves in my life, but I am quite certain that there are some racist tendencies bound up in my heart right there with tendencies to be greedy, to gossip, to lie, to be selfish, to be overly sexual, to be prideful, to be the center of attention, etc. John Piper wrote an eye-opening article on the subject of systemic racism this week, and you should read it. I don't want to be a racist. I repudiate racism in all of its forms. But I am quite sure it is there somewhere in me.

Some might say that, as a white guy, I should have no say in what words are or are not racist, and really should't write any sort of article that is critical of a man or woman of color. They might be right, and I am trying here to be wise and careful. That said, I am not sure how it is not also some form of racism for one to think that somebody's opinion is invalid because of the color of their skin – even when that color is white (or, more accurately, pinkish-white.) Yes, I could never understand racism from the point of view of somebody being racially oppressed. I suspect most people could also not understand what its like to be the parents of five kids with asthma...but that doesn't mean that I tune out all health related opinions from people who don't have kids with asthma.

As a budding writer, sometimes it is difficult to know when to write/comment about a particular subject, and when to stay away. Personally, I desire to be both somewhat provocative and irenic as a writer, but not go too far in either direction. One who is too irenic in writing often avoids any controversial topic whatsoever, and therefore never writes anything of substance or interest. Similarly, one who is overly provocative simply engages in the literary equivalent of click-bait – focusing on lots of controversy, and engendering vehement agreement or disagreement. I want to avoid both of those. Therefore, I took about a month off of writing, because, though I had much to say about the election and some very strong opinions about it – I didn't think I could say them in a way that would be particularly edifying and beneficial to readers and friends. From a writing perspective, this particular topic makes me tremble. I like LeBron James, and regularly root for him. He was my number one draft pick in fantasy basketball this year (not an auction style draft!), and I follow almost all of his games. He is an amazing player, a great athlete and a thoughtful and intelligent philanthropist. This article is not a hit piece on LeBron – I'm a fan! – but it is a very strong disagreement with his stance this week. Also – in case anybody wonders, I voted for neither Hillary nor Trump. /Virtue Signaling.

Here is Phil Jackson's comment that started the whole kerfuffle:

"It had to hurt when they lost LeBron. That was definitely a slap in the face. But there were a lot of little things that came out of that. When LeBron was playing with the Heat, they went

to Cleveland and he wanted to spend the night. They don't do overnights. Teams just don't. So now (coach Erik) Spoelstra has to text Riley and say, 'What do I do in this situation?' And Pat, who has iron-fist rules, answers, 'You are on the plane, you are with this team.' You can't hold up the whole team because you and your mom and your posse want to spend an extra night in Cleveland."

Here's is what Lebron said, in response:

"To use that label and if you go and read the definition of what the word 'posse' is, it's not what I've built over my career, It's not what I stand for, it's not what my family stands for. I believe the only reason he used that word is because he sees young African-Americans trying to make a difference. "I've been in the league for 14 years and from the beginning two years in, I felt like I wanted to put my guys in positions of power, five of those guys an opportunity to better themselves and in the beginning we were highly criticized and I was highly criticized about what I wanted to do to help some guys around me become very successful in business...It just sucks that now at this point having one of the biggest businesses you can have both on and off the floor, having a certified agent in Rich Paul, having a certified business partner in Maverick Carter, that's done so many great business, that the title for young African-Americans is the word 'posse."We see the success that we have, but then there is always someone that lets you know still how far we still have to go as African-Americans, and I don't believe that Phil Jackson would have used that term if he was doing business with someone else and working with another team or if he was working with anybody in sports that was owning a team that wasn't African-American and had a group of guys around them that didn't agree

with what they did, I don't think he would have called them a posse."

19

Appendix D: Martin Luther King Jr.

Much of the below was originally written in early 2017 on the occasion of Martin Luther King Jr. Day – I have lived all of my life in and around Birmingham, the site of many of the great feats and victories of Dr. King and the Civil Rights Struggle. I grew up in this city, born just four years after Dr. King died, and I am grateful for him, for his stance, for his leadership, and for the way he fought a terrible, evil enemy....racism...with grace and humility.

Like many great pastors and preachers of the past, (I'm thinking of Martin Luther and his views on the Jews, John Calvin and his somewhat overblown participation in the Servetus Affair, C.S. Lewis' seeming advocacy for some type of Universalism in The Last Battle, etc.), Dr. King had some theological failings. There are allegations of infidelity, and his theology can be less than biblical in several places. All of our heroes have sinful flaws – some more than others. Sometimes those flaws move somebody from the realm of Romans 7 (simultaneously sinful, yet justified), to the realm of base hypocrisy, and sometimes they don't. Honestly, I'm not always sure where that line is. At times, it is quite clear: 'Bishop' Eddie Long, who passed this week, was apparently a predatory sex offender and a certain teacher of false doctrine; that he crossed the line many times is abundantly clear. At other times, it is much less so.

Thus we are aware of the flaws of many of our heroes in this day and age. I do not believe the flaws make them more endearing. Sin is sin. My sin is ugly and disgraceful, and not the least bit charming, and so is the sin of all who have come before us. Dr. King had his flaws, but his strengths were even brighter. He was a magnificent preacher and writer. He was patient, humble and long-suffering. In the face of multiplied cruel injustices and hatreds, he managed to keep his composure and dignity and urge a whole generation of people to do the same. There was a certain explosive power in his non-violent advocacy for justice. It was not the power of a squeaky, complaining wheel demanding attention (as so many so called social justice warriors exhibit today), but the power of a passionate, uncompromising stance for righteousness that rarely, if ever, descended into unnecessary accusation, name-calling, nor antagonism.

Yes, Dr. King accorded himself with dignity, and yet HE FOUGHT. He was the furthest thing from a coward, and when he saw an America that exhibited deep symptoms of racial injustice, prejudice and pride, he rose up and fought with his words, his passion, his suffering and his life. In the face of injustice, sometimes nice people who are not brave people, just sit back and do very little – consoling themselves with the idea that their 'niceness' demands of them to not overly complain. This approach may well be appropriate when our own individual toes are being stepped on…the world could use much less complaining. However, this approach becomes cowardly in the face of systemic, ingrained brutality and justice that is harming those who cannot defend themselves. As that great English statesmen Edmund Burke wrote, "The only thing necessary for the triumph of evil is for good men to do nothing." Dr. King did the very opposite of nothing, and for that, he has my deep admiration.

Here are Ten exceptional and lesser known quotes from Dr. Martin Luther King Jr. – most of them taken from his sermons. Enjoy and be edified!

The first quote is VERY long, but so sublime that I don't believe that justice will be served by cutting it: "So American Christians, you may master the intricacies of the English language. You may possess all of the eloquence of articulate speech. But even if you "speak with the tongues of man and angels, and have not love, you are become as sounding brass, or a tinkling cymbal." You may have the gift of prophecy and understanding all mysteries. (1 Corinthians 13) You may be able to break into the storehouse of nature and bring out many insights that men never dreamed were there. You may ascend to the heights of academic achievement, so that you will have all knowledge. You may boast of your great institutions of learning and the boundless extent of your degrees. But all of this amounts to absolutely nothing devoid of love.

But even more Americans, you may give your goods to feed the poor. You may give great gifts to charity. You may tower high in philanthropy. But if you have not love it means nothing. You may even give your body to be burned, and die the death of a martyr. Your spilt blood may be a symbol of honor for generations yet unborn, and thousands may praise you as history's supreme hero. But even so, if you have not love your blood was spilt in vain. You must come to see that it is possible for a man to be self-centered in his self-denial and self-righteous in his self-sacrifice. He may be generous in order to feed his ego and pious in order to feed his pride. Man has the tragic capacity to relegate a heightening virtue to a tragic vice. Without love benevolence becomes egotism, and martyrdom becomes spiritual pride.

So the greatest of all virtues is love. It is here that we find the true meaning of the Christian faith. This is at bottom the meaning of the cross. The great event on Calvary signifies more than a meaningless drama that took place on the stage of history. It is a telescope through which we look out into the long vista of eternity and see the love of God breaking forth into time." Paul's Letter to American Christians, From a sermon preached in Montgomery, Alabama on November 11, 1956. This quote quite clearly portrays King in all his giftedness as an exceptional writer and orator. Few preachers of the last 500 years have been able to communicate with this level of eloquence. While eloquence is not the most important thing for one speaking the truth of God – "the Kingdom of God is not talk, but power" – I still admire it when I see it in a state like this.

"I don't believe meekness means that you are dried up in a very cowardly sense. But I believe it is something that gets in your soul so that you can stand and look at any man with a deep sense of humility, knowing that one day you shall inherit the earth. That's the meaning of meekness. That's what Jesus meant by it. So let us be meek and let us be humble and not go back with arrogance. Our struggle will be lost all over the South if the Negro becomes a victim of undue arrogance." Address at Holt Street Baptist Church to supporters, while celebrating the Supreme Court Ruling in Browder vs. Gayle. November, 1956

"Let us look calmly and honestly at ourselves, and we will discover that we too have those same basic desires for recognition, for importance... We all want to be important, to surpass others, to achieve distinction, to lead the parade... It's a good instinct if you don't distort it and pervert it. Don't give it up. Keep feeling the need for being important. Keep feeling the need for being first. But I want you to be first in love. (Amen) I want you to be first in moral excellence. I want you to be first in generosity.

"If you want to be important—wonderful. If you want to be recognized—wonderful. If you want to be great—wonderful. But recognize that he who is greatest among you shall be your servant. That's a new definition of greatness." - From "The Drum Major Instinct," Dr. King's final sermon, April 4, 1967.

"If physical death is the price that some must pay to free their children from a life of permanent psychological death, then nothing could be more honorable. We must somehow confront physical force with soul force and stand up courageously for justice and freedom. And this dynamic unity, this amazing self-respect, this willingness to suffer, and this refusal to hit back will cause the oppressors to become ashamed of their own methods and we will be able to transform enemies into friends." "Desegregation and the Future" Speech delivered in New York City, December 15, 1956.

"You are deeply in my prayers and thoughts as you confront arrests, threats, bombings and all types of humiliating experiences. Your wise restraint, calm dignity and unflinching courage will be an inspiration to generations yet unborn. History records nothing more majestic and sublime than the determined courage of a people willing to suffer and sacrifice for the cause of freedom. The days ahead may be difficult, but do not despair. Those of use who stand amid the bleak and desolate midnight of man's inhumanity to man must gain consolation from the fact that there is emerging a bright and glittering daybreak of freedom and justice...Remember. God lives! They that stand against him stand in a tragic and an already declared minority. They that stand with him stand in the glow of the world's bright tomorrows." December 26, 1956 letter to Birmingham Civil Rights Activist Fred Shuttlesworth.

[Our nonviolent approach] "does not seek to defeat or humiliate the opponent, but to win his friendship and understanding. The nonviolent resister must often voice his protest through non-cooperation or boycotts, but he realizes that non-cooperation and boycotts are not ends within themselves, they are merely means to awaken the sense of moral shame within the opponent. But the end is redemption. The end is reconciliation. The aftermath of nonviolence is the creation of the beloved community, while the aftermath of violence is tragic bitterness."The Christian Way of Life in Human Relations" Address delivered to the United Nations in December of 1957.

Martin Luther King Jr. Quotes

"This is what Jesus means, I think, in this very passage when he says, "Love your enemy." And it's significant that he does not say,

"Like your enemy." Like is a sentimental something, an affectionate something. There are a lot of people that I find it difficult to like. I don't like what they do to me. I don't like what they say about me and other people. I don't like their attitudes. I don't like some of the things they're doing. I don't like them. But Jesus says love them. And love is greater than like. Love is understanding, redemptive goodwill for all men, so that you love everybody, because God loves them. You refuse to do anything that will defeat an individual, because you have agape in your soul. And here you come to the point that you love the individual who does the evil deed, while hating the deed that the person does. This is what Jesus means when he says, "Love your enemy." This is the way to do it. When the opportunity presents itself when you can defeat your enemy, you must not do it." Loving Your Enemies Sermon, preached at Dexter Avenue Baptist Church in Montgomery, Alabama 1957. Generally speaking, I reject the "like" vs "love" dichotomy often discussed in our culture, but I do appreciate what Dr. King says here that even when we do not like a person's stance or behavior, that we still love the person and do not seek their 'defeating.' Many internet commentors could learn from this example!

"May I say just a word to those of you who are struggling against this evil. Always be sure that you struggle with Christian methods and Christian weapons. Never succumb to the temptation of becoming bitter. As you press on for justice, be sure to move with dignity and discipline, using only the weapon of love. Let no man pull you so low as to hate him" From a sermon preached in Montgomery, Alabama on November 11, 1956.

"One of the amazing things about the protest that will long be remembered is the orderly way it has been conducted. On every hand you have evinced wise restraint and calm dignity. You have carefully avoided animosity, making sure that your methods were rooted in the deep soils of the Christian faith. Because of this, violence has almost been a non-existent factor in our struggle. For such "discipline, generations yet unborn will commend you." December 3, 1956 address to the MIA – Montgomery Improvement Association.

"When the man in the parable knocked on his friend's door and asked for the three loaves of bread, he received the impatient retort, "Do not bother me; the door is now shut, and my children are with me in bed; I cannot get up and give you anything." How often have men experienced a similar disappointment when at midnight they knock on the door of the church. Millions of Africans, patiently knocking on the door of the Christian church where they seek the bread of social justice, have either been altogether ignored or told to wait until later, which almost always means never. Millions of American Negroes, starving for the want of the bread of freedom, have knocked again and again on the door of so-called white churches, but they have usually been greeted by a cold indifference or a blatant hypocrisy. Even the white religious leaders, who have a heartfelt desire to open the door and provide the bread, are often more cautious than courageous and more prone to follow the expedient than the ethical path. One of the shameful tragedies of history is that the very institution which should remove man from the midnight of racial segregation participates in creating and perpetuating the midnight." From a 1967 sermon entitled, "A Knock at Midnight." I agree with this charge, sadly. When the white church in the South should have stood loudly and bravely with the least of these, far too often, they turned their back.

On April 4, 1968, a "Shot rang out in the Memphis sky," and Dr. King fell mortally wounded. The day before, he had preached a sermon entitled, "I've Been to the Mountaintop." In that message, he addressed how Bull Connor and his racist Birmingham cronies had been overcome:

We aren't going to let any mace stop us. We are masters in our nonviolent movement in disarming police forces. They don't know what to do. I've seen them so often. I remember in Birmingham, Alabama, when we were in that majestic struggle there, we would move out of the Sixteenth Street Baptist Church day after day. By the hundreds we would move out, and Bull Connor would tell them to send the dogs forth, and they did come. But we just went before the dogs singing, "Ain't gonna let nobody turn me around." Bull Connor next would say, "Turn the fire hoses on." And as I said to you the other night, Bull Connor didn't know history. He knew a kind of physics that somehow didn't relate to the trans-physics that we knew about. And that was the fact that there was a certain kind of fire that no water could put out. And we went before the fire hoses. We had known water. If we were Baptist or some other denominations, we had been immersed. If we were Methodist or some others, we had been sprinkled. But we knew water. That couldn't stop us.

And we just went on before the dogs and we would look at them, and we'd go on before the water hoses and we would look at it. And we'd just go on singing, "Over my head, I see freedom in the air." (Yeah) [Applause] And then we would be thrown into paddy wagons, and sometimes we were stacked in there like sardines in a can. (All right) And they would throw us in, and old Bull would say, "Take 'em off." And they did, and we would just go on in the paddy wagon singing, "We Shall Overcome." (Yeah) And every now and then we'd get in jail, and we'd see the jailers looking through the windows being moved by our prayers (Yes) and being moved by our words and our songs. (Yes) And there was a power there which Bull Connor couldn't adjust to (All right), and so we ended up transforming Bull into a steer, and we won our struggle in Birmingham...Who is it that is supposed to articulate the longings and aspirations of the people more than the preacher? Somewhere the preacher must have a kind of fire shut up in his bones (Yes), and whenever injustice is around he must tell it. (Yes) Somehow the preacher must be an Amos, who said, "When God Speaks, who can but prophesy?" (Yes) Again with Amos, "Let justice roll down like waters and righteousness like a mighty stream." April 3, 1968 sermon, the day before Dr. King was assassinated.

This is from a Martin Luther King Jr. sermon preached in November, 1954 at Dexter Avenue Baptist Church in Montgomery, Alabama:

We know more about mathematics, about science, about social science, and philosophy, than we've ever known in any period of the world's history...For our scientific progress over the past years has been amazing. Man through his scientific genius has been able to warp distance and place time in chains, so that today it's possible to eat breakfast in New York City and supper in London, England. Back in about 1753 it took a letter three days to go from New York City to Washington, and today you can go from here to China in less time than that. It can't be because man is stagnant in his scientific progress. Man's scientific genius has been amazing.

Martin Luther King on Hate and Selfishness

I think we have to look much deeper than that if we are to find the real cause of man's problems and the real cause of the world's ills today. If we are to really find it I think we will have to look in the hearts and souls of men.

The trouble isn't so much that we don't know enough, but it's that we aren't good enough. The trouble isn't so much that our scientific genius lags behind, but our moral genius lags behind. The great problem facing modern man is that, that the means by which we live, have outdistanced the spiritual ends for which we live. So we find ourselves caught in a messed-up world. The problem is with man himself and man's soul. We haven't learned how to be just and honest and kind and true and loving. And that is the basis of our problem. The real problem is that through our scientific genius we've made of the world a neighborhood, but through our moral and spiritual genius we've failed to make of it a brotherhood. And the great danger facing us today is not so much the atomic bomb that was created by physical science. Not so much that atomic bomb that you can put in an airplane and drop on the heads of hundreds and thousands of people—as dangerous as that is. But the real danger confronting civilization today is that atomic bomb which lies in the hearts and souls of men, capable of exploding into the vilest of hate and into the most damaging selfishness. That's the atomic bomb that we've got to fear today. The problem is with the men. Within the heart and the souls of men. That is the real basis of our problem.

My friends, all I'm trying to say is that if we are to go forward today, we've got to go back and rediscover some mighty precious values that we've left behind. That's the only way that we would be able to make of our world a better world, and to make of this world what God wants it to be and the real purpose and meaning of it. The only way we can do it is to go back, and rediscover some mighty precious values that we've left behind. – Martin Luther King Jr. Dexter Avenue Baptist Church, 1954.

I believe that Martin Luther King Jr. has here rightly and eloquently diagnosed the problem with modern man: Our scientific genius is astounding, our moral genius and ability to love is...primitive. Spend five minutes browsing a contentious Facebook or Reddit discussion on politics or anything controversial, and you will see the vilest of hate and the basest of accusations. King is right about the problem. I believe he is not fully on target, however, about the cure. When he says, *"We haven't learned how to be just and honest and kind and true and loving,"* I believe he is pointing to education as the cure for our lack of love, selfish hearts, and simmering hatred. Were that true, we would expect to see a lessening of hate in the 62 plus years since King preached that sermon. However, the percentage of all races in America with high school and college degrees have shot up since then. Yes – we are more civilized. Yes, Civil Rights are light years ahead of where they were in 1954, and praise God for that. However – I would argue (based on volumes of multimedia evidence on the internet, tv and radio) that our level of hatred and selfishness has not decreased at all, but only risen. Education is good, but it does NOT produce heart change. I believe it is the good news of Jesus – the Gospel – that brings transformation to hearts and ways of thinking.

Here is Tim Keller, writing in his book The Prodigal God, explaining this dynamic:

It is only when you see the desire to be your own Savior and Lord -lying beneath both your sins and your moral goodness- that you are on the verge of understanding the gospel and becoming a Christian indeed. When you realize that the antidote to being bad is not just being good, you are on the brink. If you follow through, it will change everything: how you relate to God, self, others, the world, your work, your sins, your virtue. It's called the new birth because it's so radical. (p. 78) Jesus Christ, who had all the power in the world, saw us enslaved by the very things we thought would free us. So he emptied himself of his glory and became a servant. He laid aside the infinities and immensities of his being and, at the cost of his life, paid the debt for our sins, purchasing us the only place our hearts can rest, in his Father's house... Knowing this will transform us from the inside out... Why wouldn't you want to offer yourself to someone like this? Selfless love destroys the mistrust in our hearts toward God that makes us either younger brothers or elder brothers... We will never stop being younger brothers of elder brothers until we acknowledge our need, rest by faith, and gaze in wonder at the work of our true elder brother, Jesus Christ. – Tim Keller, Prodigal God, 2008.

"And I wonder why it is that the forces of evil seem to reign supreme and the forces of goodness seem to be trampled over. Every now and then I feel like asking God, Why is it that over so many centuries the forces of injustice have triumphed over the Negro and he has been forced to live under oppression and slavery and exploitation? Why is it, God? Why is it simply because some of your children ask to be treated as first-class human beings they are trampled over, their homes are bombed, their children are pushed from their classrooms, and sometimes little children [referencing Emmett

Till] are thrown in the deep waters of Mississippi? Why is it, oh God, that that has to happen? I begin to despair sometimes, it seems that Good Friday has the throne. It seems that the forces of injustice reign supreme. But then in the midst of that something else comes to me." – Martin Luther King Jr. 1957 Easter Sermon in Montgomery, Alabama, "Questions that Easter Answers."

The Outrageous and Tragic Death Of Emmett Till.

During the Summer of 2016, I gathered our older children in the kitchen and told them the tragic and infuriating story of Emmett Till, a fourteen year old African American boy who was brutally lynched in 1955 for the 'crime' of talking to a young married woman whom he had just purchased candy from. To my knowledge, it was the first that my kids had heard of Emmett Till, a fact which I, as a history teacher responsible for their education, feel quite saddened by. They should have known about Emmett Till before now. Maybe you don't know about Emmett either? Or maybe you've heard the name before, but are hazy on the details of his story. Here's what happened, why it is trending on Twitter today*** (scroll to the bottom), and a little bit about the radical person who called for forgiveness for the murderers of young Emmett.

In August of 1955, Emmett Till, a young teenager from Chicago, was visiting relatives in Money, Mississippi, a tiny (400 population at the time) town in the Delta area in the middle of the state. Till and a few friends skipped church one Sunday morning, and went to Bryant's Grocery store in Money to purchase some candy. While at the store, Till allegedly showed some of his friends that accompanied him a picture of his school class in Chicago, which was integrated, featuring white and black students in the same classroom. This, along with Till's statement that he had white friends, was shocking to his companions in the segregated south, who may (or may not...) have challenged him to talk with Carolyn Bryant, the 21 year old shopkeeper that was tending to Bryant's Grocery store that morning. Later, Carolyn Bryant apparently told her husband and some other relatives that Emmett had flirted with her, testifying later in court that he had grabbed her hand and said, "How about a date, baby?"*** This testimony, later proved to be a LIE, so incensed Bryant's husband Roy, and his half brother J.W. Milam, that they went and found Emmett, kidnapped him from his preacher Uncle, tortured him, and killed him. A FOURTEEN year old boy. Witnesses later testified that Till was heard to cry out, "Mama, Lord have mercy...Lord have mercy," as he was being beaten to death. Till was shot in the head, brutally beaten all over his body, and his eye was dislodged from his socket when he was found and pulled from a river, where he had been tied to a 75 pound piece of metal, and drowned.

Ultimately, Milam and Bryant were arrested and charged with murder. There was little hope of a conviction, however, in 1950s Mississippi. Indeed, a week before Till had arrived in town, Civil Rights activist Lamar Smith had been gunned down in front of a courthouse in Brookhaven, and his white killers would end up judged not guilty. Similarly, Milam and Bryant were acquitted – primarily due to the defense claims that it couldn't conclusively be proved that the body pulled from the Tallahatchie River, was the body of Emmett Till. Reading the circumstances of the trial, however, one comes away with the belief that justice was miscarried to an extreme degree. Sheriff Strider, the chief lawman in Money who had arrested and jailed two key prosecution eyewitnesses to keep them from testifying, was said to have greeted African-Americans that came to watch the five day trial with a cheerful, "Hello, N***rs!" Strider, an evil, almost caricatured version of the racist Southern lawman, also threatened those around the country who had sent his office letters of critique, threatening that if they ever came to Mississippi, "the same thing's gonna happen to them that happened to Emmett Till"

Sherriff Strider, delivering a legal document to Emmett Till's mother.

Further, the all white jurors were allowed to drink beer during the court proceedings, and many of the white spectators came armed with guns to the trial, which surely had an intimidating effect. Thus it is very unsurprising that the jury voted to acquit both men after deliberating for just over an hour. One juror noted that it could have even been a shorter deliberation, "If we hadn't stopped to drink pop, it wouldn't have taken that long." Subsequently, after the trial, it was shown that most of the jurors did, in fact, believe that Bryant and Milam were guilty, but that the potential sentence for their crime – death or life in prison – was too harsh of a punishment for a white man who killed a black child. (SOURCE for both statements)

Courtroom at Emmett Till Trial

That justice was miscarried is indisputable. Both Bryant and Milam, admitted their guilt in a 1956 interview, knowing they would not be punished for it due to the American legal principle of double jeopardy. In that interview in Look Magazine, Milam offered up this hateful assessment:

"I'm no bully; I never hurt a ni***r in my life. I like ni***rs—in their place—I know how to work 'em. But I just decided it was time a few people got put on notice. As long as I live and can do anything about it, ni***rs are gonna stay in their place. Ni***rs ain't gonna vote where I live. If they did, they'd control the government. They ain't gonna go to school with my kids. And when a ni***r gets close to mentioning sex with a white woman, he's tired o' livin'. I'm likely to kill him. Me and my folks fought for this country, and we got some rights. I stood there in that shed and listened to that ni***r throw that poison at me, and I just made up my mind. 'Chicago boy,' I said, 'I'm tired of 'em sending your kind down here to stir up trouble. God**m you, I'm going to make an example of you—just so everybody can know how me and my folks stand."

Roy Bryant and J.W. Milam defense team.

It can be said, with an appropriate degree of sadness, anger and hope, that Emmett Till did not die in vain. I am not terribly comfortable with that sentence, so perhaps I can word it in a somewhat different way: Emmett Till's death, as tragic as it was, had the remarkable impact of igniting and energizing the Civil Rights Movement in a very galvanizing way. Till's mother made the difficult decision to have an open casket funeral for her son. There are pictures available for this, but as important as they are historically, I think I am going to avoid putting them here. The funeral for Till – with his disfigured corpse on full display – caused an outcry among many in the United States, and helped to unite several factions that had been separately striving for civil rights. It was eye-opening for many American whites to realize the depths of racism found in America, and even a majority of people in and around Money, Mississippi utterly rejected Roy Bryant and J.W. Milam, forcing them to move to Texas, where they were equally unpopular. Emmett Till's unjust death also served as a strong inspiration for Rosa Parks, the Montgomery bus rider who refused to give up her seat.

Mamie Till Bradley, Emmett Till's mother, grieves at her son's funeral.

"Mississippi became in the eyes of the nation the epitome of racism and the citadel of white supremacy. From this time on, the slightest racial incident anywhere in the state was spotlighted and magnified. To the Negro race throughout the South and to some extent in other parts of the country, this verdict indicated an end to the system of noblesse oblige. The faith in the white power structure waned rapidly. Negro faith in legalism declined, and the revolt officially began on December 1, 1955, with the Montgomery, Alabama, bus boycott." –

Historian Stephen Whittaker

SO – what should our response to the death of Emmett Till be? How should society respond to the revelation that Carolyn Bryant FABRICATED and LIED about the whole incident? Should she be arrested for inciting this murder? Perhaps so. What Bryant did is astonishingly inexcusable. There is no acceptable reason or excuse she can use to justify herself. Less so, there is neither reason nor justification for the brutal actions of J.W. Milam and Roy Bryant and all of the other purveyors of racial atrocities, like Bull Connor, Byron De La Beckwith, James Earl Ray, and the murderers of Chaney, Goodman and Schwerner. Those men are rightly vilified. But...should they be forgiven? Should forgiveness be offered for those who have committed extreme acts of violence and racism, or – as many on Twitter and other social media are suggesting – should people like Carolyn Bryant and her ilk "rot in hell," because what they've done is beyond forgiveness? I don't think so. In fact, I don't think anything, in light of Jesus and His death on the cross, is beyond forgiveness for all who would look to Him in faith believing. However, I realize the peril of me – a white man who has never been the victim of racial prejudice – calling for forgiveness for egregious racists and past acts of racism. No, I'm not going to call for those people to be forgiven, but I do have a few quotes to share, in closing. These are quotes from a well known radical of past years. A man whom many considered crazy, uppity and dangerous in his day. That man, Martin Luther King Jr., actually had a lot to say about the death of Emmett Till, and how we should treat his killers:

Bennett College Newspaper Interviewer: "Doctor King, I have just a few questions. Now you talk about forgiveness and that you must forgive. Do you find that really in your heart you can forgive the men who, say, killed Emmett Till or castrated this innocent man? And don't you find it really hard..."

[King:] [interrupting] Well, if you really love on the basis of

Christian concepts, forgiveness is very difficult. It isn't easy. And when it becomes so easy it really isn't forgiveness. There is pain and agony. A husband who loves his wife or vice versa, when one makes a tragic mistake, they can't forgive easy. But it's possible. And when I say forgiving I don't mean that this is something weak or this is something, just a sentimental sort of thing. I think ultimately it is the only [normal?] method of reconciliation. Whether it's in social life, or whether it's in individual relations. It's very difficult and it's very hard not to become bitter toward such persons. But forgiveness has great psychological value. Not only does it have healing social power but it has psychological power. If I'm bitter toward a man it hurts me as much as it hurts him. And I think psychologists are telling us today that hate not only hurts the hated but it hurts the hater as much. So for me not to forgive the people who killed Emmett Till or the people who mutilated the man in Birmingham, I am setting in my very personality a structure of evil which can cause a disintegration in my personality." (Dr. King is speaking of those who murdered Emmett Till and those Ku Klux Klan men who castrated and tortured Judge Edward Aaron, a developmentally disabled African American man in Birmingham, Alabama.

Let me close this story with the conclusion of the Martin Luther King Jr. quote that I began with – the ending of his message that referenced the power of evil in the death of Till and the greater power of love, forgiveness and Jesus:

You know every now and then, my friends, I doubt. Every now and then I get disturbed myself. Every now and then I become bewildered about this thing. I begin to despair every now and then. And wonder why it is that the forces of evil seem to reign supreme and the forces of goodness seem to be trampled over. Every now and then I feel like asking God, Why is it that over so many centuries the forces of injustice have triumphed over the Negro and he has been forced to live under oppression and slavery and exploitation? Why is it, God? Why is it simply because some of your children ask to be treated as first-class human beings they are trampled over, their homes are bombed, their children are pushed from their classrooms, and sometimes little children are thrown in the deep waters of Mississippi?16 Why is it, oh God, that that has to happen? I begin to despair sometimes, it seems that Good Friday has the throne. It seems that the forces of injustice reign supreme. But then in the midst of that something else comes to me.

And I can hear something saying, "King, you are stopping at Good Friday, but don't you know that Easter is coming? (Yeah) Don't worry about this thing! You are just in the midst of the transition now. You are just in the midst of Good Friday now. But I want you to know, King, that Easter is coming! One day truth will rise up and reign supreme! (Yeah) One day justice will rise up. One day all of the children of God will be able to stand up on the third day and then cry, 'Hallelujah, Hallelujah' (Yeah) because it's the Resurrection day." (That's the truth)

And when I hear that I don't despair. I can cry out and sing with new meaning. This is the meaning of Easter, it answers the profound question that we confront in Montgomery. And if we can just stand with it, if we can just live with Good Friday, things will be all right. For I know that Easter is coming and I can see it coming now. As I look over the world, as I look at America, I can see Easter coming in race relations. I can see it coming on every hand. I see it coming in Montgomery. I see it coming in Alabama. I see it coming in Mississippi. Sometimes it looks like it's coming slow, but it's still coming. (Yeah) And when it comes, it will be a great day, for all of the children of God will be able to stand up and cry, "This is God's day. All hail the power of Jesus's name." This is the meaning of it.

...[the most durable power in the world is] the power of love. Easter tells us that. Sometimes it looks like the other powers are much more durable. Then we come to see that isn't true. But the most durable, lasting power in this world is the power to love...

And I watched Jesus as he walked around the hills of Galilee just doing good, just preaching the gospel to the brokenhearted, healing the sick and raising the dead. And I just watched him. I looked at him, and I said, "Now, he doesn't have a band [following him?] He has no great army! He has no great military power." Then I can see him go with another kind of army. I can hear him as he says somehow to himself, "I'm just going to put on the breastplate of righteousness. And I'm going take the ammunition of love and the whole armor of God, and I'm just gonna march." And my friends, he started marching. And after he marched a little while, he came to his Waterloo. Good Friday came, and there he was on the cross. T

hat was his Waterloo. But the difference is that Napoleon's Waterloo ended with Waterloo. Jesus's Waterloo ended transforming Waterloo. (Amen) And there came that third day. And this was the [time?] that he was able to reign supreme. His Waterloo couldn't stop him. He stopped Waterloo. And this became the beginning of his influence. This became the most powerful moment of his life. [As?] I walked away from that building, I could hear choirs singing everywhere.

On this side, it seemed that I could hear somebody saying:

All hail the power of Jesus's name!

Let angels prostrate fall, (That's the truth)

Bring forth the royal diadem,

And crown him Lord of all.

We thank you, this morning, for your Son, Jesus, who came by to let us know that love is the most durable power in the world, who came by to let us know that death can't defeat us, to take the sting out of the grave and death and make it possible for all of us to have eternal life." Martin Luther King Jr. Easter, 1957 sermon at Dexter Avenue Baptist Church

*** The reason that Emmett Till is trending today [editor's note: written during the Summer of 2016) on social media is because Carolyn Bryant, who is still alive and in her 80s, has been interviewed for a new book by Timothy Tyson about the Emmett Till murder. In that book, Tyson recounts that Bryant has completely recanted her story that Till made verbal and physical advances towards her. She can't remember the details of anything that happened that day, but she admits she fabricated – LIED – about the most sensational facts of the case. Frustratingly, it would appear that while Ms. Bryant seems to regret what happened, she evidences little repentance for her role in the murder of Emmett Till. That is tragic, but let me be crystal CLEAR. There is absolutely NOTHING in the Bible that discourages relationships between white people and black people in any way, shape, or form. If Till HAD made advances towards Ms. Bryant, which he obviously did NOT, he might have been guilty of being fresh, or something in that realm, but nothing more! Yes, the Israelites were prohibited in the Bible to marry people from nations that followed foreign Gods, but that was a RELIGIOUS prohibition, in the OLD Covenant, that directly applied to ISRAELITES – not Gentiles. (Gentiles are all of those who are not of Israelite blood – Americans, Africans, Asians, etc.) There is NOTHING, NOTHING, NOTHING in the Bible that suggests that white people and black people should not be in relationship, married or otherwise. It is the vile racism to the core, and extreme biblical ignorance to argue otherwise. If you believe that people of different races shouldn't get married then that is your opinion, and it is a very WRONGHEADED one, but it is not an opinion based on the Bible, or the will of God in any way. Please don't do what many racists in the past have done: twist the Bible to justify your sin.

Contact Information and Thank you!

If you are interested in reading more of my books, please go to my website, www.Chaseathompson.com, and click on the 'contact' link. I would love to add you to my newsletter, and all you have to do to be included is just send me a message through my website, or use my personal email address: Chaseathompson@gmail.com. I won't spam you, and I won't send you emails very often, but I will, from time to time, send you free offers and news about new book releases.

If you are interested in more of my work – including the next few volumes in the WTBRS (What the Bible REALLY Says) Series, please check out my author page on Amazon.com (https://www.amazon.com/Chase-Thompson/e/B06Y16M3Q3/) Or visit my webpage: www.Chaseathompson.com/blog